The Articles Treated on in Tract 90 Reconsidered
by Edward Bouverie Pusey

Address:
HardPress
8345 NW 66TH ST #2561
MIAMI FL 33166-2626
USA
Email: info@hardpress.net

THE

ARTICLES

TREATED ON IN TRACT 90

RECONSIDERED

AND THEIR INTERPRETATION

VINDICATED

IN A LETTER

TO THE

REV. R. W. JELF, D.D.

CANON OF CHRIST CHURCH.

WITH AN APPENDIX FROM ABP. USSHER ON THE DIFFERENCE BETWEEN
ANCIENT AND MODERN ADDRESSES TO SAINTS.

———

BY THE

REV. E. B. PUSEY, D.D.

REGIUS PROFESSOR OF HEBREW, CANON OF CHRIST CHURCH,
LATE FELLOW OF ORIEL COLLEGE.

———

OXFORD,

JOHN HENRY PARKER;

J. G. F. AND J. RIVINGTON, LONDON.

1841.

1017.

BAXTER, PRINTER, OXFORD.

CONTENTS.

My Dear Friend,

The deep interest which you have ever taken in all which concerns the well-being of our Church, both when serving her, away from your home, in aiding to form (under God) a valuable character which may be, by His blessing, of importance to thousands, and more recently, since you have been restored to us, leaves me no doubt that you will gladly allow yourself again to be addressed on the subject, out of which so much agitation has recently been raised. And this the rather, since, although you have uniformly from the first held " that form of doctrine which was delivered" to us, and wherein your mind was moulded, you have, by your absence, been detached from the efforts of those who have been of late endeavouring to restore it to others, and so also, from the imperfections, infirmities, or errors, which may have clung to any of us in the execution of our task. Agreeing with us as to our general principles on the authority of the Church, the value of " Catholic consent" as a guide to the meaning of Holy Scripture, the high dignity of the Sacraments, the necessity of a higher

B

standard of holiness, self-denial, self-discipline, almsgiving, than has of late been common among us, you are not committed to any thing which we have said on these subjects in detail. You are come among us, I hope, to assist, under God's guidance,—separately, yet one in heart and object, —in the restoration of a higher sense of our privileges and duties as members and Ministers of the Apostolic Church of this land.

Nor would I, by any thing I write, seek to identify you with myself; enough that we are bound by the privileges of our common duty, and the friendship of most of our lives hitherto.

Nor, again, do I wish to enter into a vindication of the Tract, which has been the centre of this excitement. That, I am convinced, is best left in the hands of its writer; nor do I wish to make him, who views things far more deeply than I can, responsible for my construction of its details. I wish only to help to relieve, if I may, the perplexity of some minds, who think principles which they hold, involved in the censure passed upon the Tract, as also the anxieties of another class, who fear lest the adoption of the principles therein inculcated, should lead to a relaxation of the mode in which the Articles are subscribed. As an instance of this perplexity, I may mention, that calm and conscientious persons have been seriously perplexed, whether they could retain their offices, as Tutors, after the sentence of condemnation passed on the Tract by the Heads of Houses. In this place, where the advice of elders can easily be had, such could readily be reassured, that the sense in which they understood the Tract, and consequently the way in which they subscribed and explained the Articles, was not that which the Heads of Houses meant to condemn. The perplexity however would be much more extensive and embarrassing, if any of our Bishops should hereafter advert to the Tract, and, without explaining their own views, seem to countenance the general condemnation by the Heads; among those, who coincide with the real views of the Tract, are many by whom the slightest word of their Bishop would be deeply felt; and who yet would find a difficulty in explaining themselves to him ; circumstances, to which I need not here advert, have added to the distance at which a Presbyter must naturally feel himself removed from his Bishop; such persons would naturally too shrink from wearying their already overburthened Bishop with explanations, which would necessarily require much detail, and exhibition of their own personal feelings and views. '' Why speakest thou any more of thy matters ?" would be the feeling of such persons. And thus they would seem left to decide, as they best might, whether they could continue to serve in a Diocese in which their views of the Articles, on subscribing which they had been admitted to their cure, seemed to have been censured, whether it might not give scandal, even if otherwise allowable, whether they ought not silently to withdraw, and yet whether such withdrawing would not be a tacit admission, that the sense in which they had hitherto signed the Articles was an " evasion." On these and other grounds, valuable persons, whose labours our Church could ill spare, might be much harassed, if a Bishop should, by any unexplained reference to the censure of the Heads, seem to lay down that the Articles could not be conscientiously signed on the principles of the Tract, whereas such would, in fact, sign them or adhere to them, not on the principles objected to, but on such, as would be recognized by their Bishops themselves. On the other hand, I have had reason to know, that one chief fear of those who have blamed the Tract, has been lest it should introduce lax ways of signing the Articles generally, or sanction their being signed by persons, who had parted even with the most essential truths which they embody.

On these grounds, I examined (as I was able) the Tract itself, with the view to ascertain what was the amount of the relaxation of the Articles involved in it. It is the result of that examination with which I am now going to trouble you.

Some of the causes, which may have led to misapprehension, the Author of the Tract has, with that simplicity and candour which we so well know, mentioned to yourself in his Letter to you, and its Postscript. But what I wish to draw attention to is something distinct. The Author had, apparently, two objects in view; one, to vindicate the Catholic interpretation of the Articles against a modern popular system of interpreting them, and to shew that our Articles, fairly construed, were in no case opposed to any teaching of the Church Catholic ; secondly, to shew, that certain opinions or practices, which, *though not Catholic*, are to be found more or less prevalent in the early centuries, may yet be held as private opinions by individuals, without hindering any from signing the Articles with a safe conscience. In few words, that *our Articles neither contradict any thing Catholic, nor are meant to condemn any thing in early Christianity, even though not Catholic, but only the later definite system in the Church of Rome.* Perhaps these two points would be better elicited without reference to the Tridentine decrees, since this part of the question relates rather to the hope of the future repentance and restoration of Rome, than to any thing which concerns ourselves at this moment.

Now it appears to me, 1st, that the proposed interpretation of the Articles relates almost entirely to the first of these two points, on which no question would be raised, at least by none, except those of extreme views ; 2dly, that there is so broad a line between any practices or doctrines occurring any where in earlier Christianity, and any later corruptions in the Church of Rome, that there is no grounds whatever to think that the framers of the Articles, in condemning the latter, had any view to the former. I cannot then but think, that apart from the construction which has been put upon expressions in the Tract, its main, real, principles will be acknowledged, at once or gradually, to be true.

The point which I have put second, is necessarily matter of detail. The first, as I have stated it, (and it alone is of essential moment,) was, I conceive, never objected to, although it would seem to be included in the general condemnation of " the modes of interpretation suggested by the Tract."

For it would be generally admitted, except by those trained in a modern school, that any particular Church owes obedience to the Universal Church, of which it is a part; that what can be proved to have been universally received in the primitive ages, is more likely to be true than any view promulgated by individuals in modern times ; that what in times near to the Apostles was universally received by the Church, is more likely to be Apostolic, than any system formed now. For myself, you are aware, I hold much more than this, and, with the current of our great Divines, believe that what in early ages can be proved, according to the rule of Vincentius, to have been held " every where, at all times, and by all," is, if matter of doctrine, binding still. But

at the least, such a principle would not be condemned by those who hold the chairs of Laud,
Jackson, and Fell, or in the University of
Hooker, Sanderson, Hammond, and Bull. Considering the reverence which our Church has
ever paid to Christian Antiquity, the mode in
which our Homilies join its teaching with that of
Holy Scripture itself[a], and in which the Convocation, which inforced subscription to the Articles,
refers us to it, as our guide to the doctrine of those
Scriptures[b]; considering, again, the reception of the
four or six first General Councils, the directions
obtained by our Bishops for the studies of this very
University[c], the tone which has prevailed among

[a] e. g. " contrary to the most manifest doctrine of the Scriptures, and contrary to the usage of the Primitive Church, which
was most pure and uncorrupt, and contrary to the sentences of
the most ancient, learned, and godly doctors of the Church."
Quoted Tract 90, p. 70. n. 10. " being warned by God's holy
word, and by the writings of the old godly doctors and ecclesiastical historians." ib. no. 22. add nos. 23. 27. 43. 45. 50. 51.

[b] " They [preachers] shall in the first place be careful never
to teach any thing from the pulpit to be religiously held and
believed by the people, but what is agreeable to the doctrine of
the Old and New Testament, and collected out of that very doctrine by the Catholic Fathers and ancient Bishops." Canons of
1571.

[c] " Let young Students of Theology be directed to study such
books as be most agreeable in doctrine and discipline to the
Church of England ; and incited to bestow their times in the
Fathers, the Councils, Schoolmen, Histories, and Controversies ;
and not to insist too long on compendiums and abbreviatures,
making them the grounds of their study in Divinity."
" 7th Direction which the most wise King James, (A. D.

her great Divines, it is little to say that her present Heads could not have meant to have prescribed to the Tutors of their respective Colleges to expound the Articles according to the private interpretations of modern schools, or the supposed opinions of the framers, in contradistinction to the teaching of Catholic Antiquity.

But yet further, the framers of our Articles themselves had no such wish.   Our Reformers did not wish that we should be Cranmerites or Ridleyans; they did not wish to stamp their own image and superscription upon our portion of God's Church ; whatever imperfections they may as men have been subject to, they wished only to clear the fine gold from any tarnish which had come over it ; we have remained since the Reformation, as before, a branch of the Church Catholic ; we were placed on no new platform ; our Reformers did not, like Luther, form for us any new system of doctrine, such as that which bears his name ; they ever appealed to Catholic Antiquity ; submitted their own judgment to hers.   " To depart," says Bishop Ridley, " from that the sentences of the old ancient writers do more allow, without any warrant of God's word, I cannot think it any Godly wisdom."   And even Cranmer, at a very solemn

1617.) *by the advice of the Bishops,* addressed to the University of Oxford, the Vice-Chancellor, the Governors of Colleges and Halls, the two Professors, to be by them diligently observed." *Bp. Bull, Apologia pro Harmonia, S.* 1. §. 4.

moment [c], professed his readiness " in all things to follow the judgment of the most sacred word of God and of the holy Catholic Church." And confessed,

" In all my doctrine and preaching both of the Sacraments, and of other my doctrine, whatsoever it be, not only I mean and judge, as the Catholic Church and the most holy Fathers of old meant and judged, but also, I would gladly use the same words that they used and not any other words; but to set my hand to all and singular their speeches, phrases, ways, and forms of speech, which they do use in their treatises upon the Sacraments, and to keep still their interpretation."

It were, also, manifestly, a grievous yoke, and such as it has not been ever attempted formally to lay upon us, so to tie us down to the opinions of (to use a favourite expression of a modern school) " fallible men," that we should be compelled to search up and down the works of the Reformers in order to expound the Articles according to their insight into Divine truth, and to take, as authoritative, all which, in the perplexity of controversy, may have dropped from them. The difficulty of ascertaining the meaning of Catholic Antiquity is sometimes urged by the opponents of its authority as an argument against its use; yet its language in matters of faith is clear and definite; but what a task were it to turn us adrift in writings, whose authors on some points

[c] Appeal at his degradation, Works, vol. iv. p. 126, 7.

confessedly changed their views; who had a difficulty in fixing their language, lest while avoiding
prevalent errors, they should unsettle kindred
truth; who were embarrassed by all that perplexity, which any change of rooted opinions, for
the time, almost of necessity, involves; who were
surrounded by opposing errors; were, in some
degree, joined in one common cause of removing
abuses with men, like the Swiss Reformers, themselves involved in grievous error, and so must and did
sympathize with them, and wished to mould them
with themselves in one Reformed Church [d]. If
it be thought difficult in Christian Antiquity to
separate what is Catholic from what may be peculiar to the mind of the writer, what a task were it
to take the works of such a period as this, for the
rule of our theological teaching !

. Again, (as has been often stated,) we have not our
Articles from their framers; the Forty-two Articles
of Edward VI. were never accepted by the Church
at large [e]; though mainly the same, they were still
modified, when formed into the Thirty-nine; primitive and essential words of our Liturgy were
then restored; our Services were then, in expression certainly, restored to a more primitive
mould than under the Reformers; why then is
our Church to be bound to go back to the Re-

[d] See Tract 81, p. 27. note on the origin of the Forty-two
Articles.

[e] Strype's Cranmer, ii. 27, 34. Heylyn, p. 121.

formers, for the exposition of Articles, which in their present forms he did not receive from them, and whose work in other respects she reformed upon the primitive model ?

The last Convocation from which we received them, was at a period (1662) when the deference owed to Catholic Antiquity, which the Reformers felt, was most fully developed and understood.

One needed not to have used many words on this subject but for a recent tendency to set up the Reformers—not as instruments only of God's good Providence in removing error, but—as the founders of a system of faith, and the authorized expositors of our belief. This is the real point at issue, of which there were other indications before this controversy arose. Men must lean upon some authority; they cannot guide themselves ; they who think they derive their faith immediately and exclusively from Holy Scripture, for the most part follow human guidance more rigidly than others ; the only real question is, from whom, under God's guidance, we shall learn the meaning of those Scriptures, from ancients or from moderns.

Whatever then individuals may practise for themselves, it will not, I conceive, be generally objected to any of us, as a grave error, that we hold that the Articles are to be interpreted according to the teaching of the Church Catholic. Let me then request you, as briefly as may be, to go through with me the several Articles relating to the points

in controversy between us and the Romanists, and
so see whether the main objects of the Tract be not
what I have said. If, even on points of doctrine or
practice not-Catholic, there be a distinct line between what is early and what is Romanist, it will,
of course, be no relaxation of the Articles to maintain, that when they speak of what is " Romish,"
they do not contemplate any thing in early Christianity ; on the other hand, in what forms, as we
shall see, the main object of the Tract—to shew on
points, where there is a Catholic doctrine, that our
Articles are in harmony with the teaching of the
Church Catholic ;—this view, so far from relaxing
the meaning of the Articles, gives them greater
stringency, and lays us under a deeper obligation ;
since now we are bound to receive them not only
on the authority of our immediate mother, but of
her, " the Jerusalem from above, who is the" common " mother of us all."

Articles vi. and xx.

" Holy Scripture and the Authority of the Church.

" Holy Scripture containeth all things necessary to
salvation ; so that whatsoever is not read therein, nor may
be proved thereby, is not to be required of any man, that
it should be believed as an article of the Faith, or be thought
requisite or necessary to salvation. . . . . .The Church hath
power to decree (statuendi) rites and ceremonies, and authority in controversies of faith ; and yet it is not lawful
for the Church to ordain (instituere) any thing that is contrary to God's word written, neither may it so expound

one place of Scripture, that it be repugnant to another. Wherefore, although the Church be a witness and a keeper of Holy Writ, yet as it ought not to decree (decernere) any thing against the same, so besides the same, ought it not to enforce (obtrudere) any thing to be believed for necessity of salvation."

With regard to these two Articles, little has been done except to combine their teaching; an Ultra-Protestant sense can only be given to the sixth Article by detaching it from the twentieth. Alone, it only *declares*, what is the *source* of the articles of faith, Holy Scripture; how those articles are to be derived from that source, is *implied* only; it stands over against the Romanist system, which requires things to be believed as articles of faith, which are " not read in Holy Scripture nor can be proved by it :" who is so to prove it, who has the power of " requiring" what can be so proved, to be believed as an Article of the Faith, is reserved for the twentieth. Only, (as observed elsewhere,) in speaking of " requiring," it *implies* that some one has the right to require; and that right the twentieth declares to be vested in the Church; " the Church has authority in controversies of faith." The same Article implies that the Church has a right to " expound Scripture" and " enforce things to be believed, which can be proved thereby ;" for it were idle to say that " it is not lawful for the Church *so* to expound one place of Scripture, that it be repugnant to another," unless, within these

limits she were its lawful expositor ; or to say that
" besides Holy Writ, she ought not to enforce
any thing to be believed for necessity of salvation,"
unless out of Holy Writ she might so enforce
them.   And this power of the Church we ourselves practically acknowledge whenever we repeat
the Athanasian Creed.

This the Tract sums up thus :

" First, the Church *expounds and enforces the faith ;*
for it is forbidden to expound in a particular way, or so
to enforce as to obtrude ; next, that it derives the faith
wholly from Scripture ; third, that its office is to educe an
harmonious interpretation of Scripture."

Indeed, the Tract, so far from pressing, as I
think it might, that in points of faith, or things
necessary to salvation, " private judgment" is
excluded, contents itself with saying that it is at
least an open question ; " nothing is said [in the
Article] of the *private judgment of the individual*
being the ultimate standard of interpretation :" nor
on the other does it assert any thing as to catholic
tradition being the Church's guide in interpreting
Holy Scripture, but only negatively that " not a
word is said in favour of Scripture having no rule
or method to fix interpretation by, or, as is commonly expressed, *being the sole rule of faith.*"   So
that, so far from drawing the Article to any extreme
view, our friend only shews that it does not contain
any thing contradicting the authority of the Church
and tradition, leaving others free possession of

their opinion, provided that they ascribe not to the Article un-Catholic statements, to which it is rather opposed. At the same time, he maintains fully against the Romish error, that the faith is derived " *wholly from Scripture*," discarding only the term " sole rule of faith" as ambiguous. For where Scripture is by moderns termed " the sole rule of faith," it is used in the sense of the sole " source of faith," or the sole " ultimate standard of faith," as opposed to any other independent documents of the Faith ; where the title " rule of faith" is given to the Creeds, it means the rule whereby the soundness of the faith of individuals or Churches may be tested. Scripture is the rule of the Creeds ; the Creeds, of the faith of individuals or particular Churches.

Since, however, any mention of tradition is thought to favour errors in the Church of Rome, (often as it has been shewn that those errors do not rest upon Tradition but are opposed to it,) it may be well to set down some words of Thorndike[f], shewing that any reliance upon it is in fact opposed to the doctrine of infallibility, as on the other hand any appeal to human authorities is to that of Scripture being the sole guide to the faith.

" Always it is easy for me to demonstrate that this resolution, ' That the Scripture, holding the meaning of it by the tradition of the Church, is the only means to decide controversies of Faith,' is nearer to the common terms, that the Scripture is the only rule of faith, than to that infallibility which is pretended for the Church

[f] Epilogue i. 32. p. 196.

of Rome; having demonstrated, that, to depend upon the infallibility of the present, and the tradition of the Catholic Church, are things inconsistent, whereas this cannot be inconsistent with that Scripture, which is no less delivered from age to age than tradition is, though the one by writing, the other by word of mouth, and serving chiefly to determine the true meaning of it, when it comes in debate."

And a little before;

" For as I have argued, that those who maintain the infallibility of the present Church, do contradict themselves, whensoever they have recourse either to the Scripture or to any words of the Church, to evidence the sense of the Scripture in that, which otherwise they profess the authority of the Church alone infallibly to determine: so, those who will have the Scripture alone to determine all controversies of faith, and yet take the pains to bring evidence of the meaning thereof, from that which had been received in the Church, may very well be said to contradict themselves."

With the same moderation is the subject of the "Apocrypha" touched upon; and as the Author has since stated, it has been one source of the imputation of vagueness cast upon the Tract, that he did not wish to press his own conclusions, but only negatively to secure a fair liberty for those for whom he wrote, against un-Catholic interpretations, which a popular system would identify with the Articles.

It is needless to say to you how deeply some persons, mostly but little acquainted with the Apocrypha, condemn it, how they offend foreign

Churches by translating and circulating the Bible without it, how they would gladly displace it from the order of our Lessons, how they have in fact succeeded in removing it from the Bible in ordinary circulation among us. In opposition to this, the Tract states, p. 6.

" that the books which are commonly called Apocrypha, are not asserted in this Article to be destitute of inspiration or to be simply human, but to be not canonical; in other words, to differ from Canonical Scripture, specially in this respect, viz. that they are not adducible in proof of doctrine. ' The other books (as Hierome saith) the Church doth read for example of life and instruction of manners, and yet doth not apply them to establish any doctrine.'"

It might have said much more; and our Church, in this as in other instances, by taking up the position of the early Church, takes away the vantage-ground of Romish Controversialists. For these, in opposition to such as deny the Apocrypha any value, or look upon it as a mere human book, can easily appeal to its being read in Churches together with the Canonical Scriptures, or to passages of the fathers, in which they cite from it, under the title of " Scripture, Divine Scripture," and the like. The subject is far too wide to adduce the proof thus incidentally ; yet I may mention as the result of a long and careful investigation, that I found full evidence that no other Canon of the Old Testament as possessing *plenary* Inspiration, was

ever received in any Church, than that of the
Hebrew Scriptures ; and yet, that the same fathers,
who were fully aware of this, did, in every Church,
without scruple, cite the Apocryphal books of the
Old Testament, as being in a sense inspired beyond
the writings of any men after the Apostolic age.
They do indeed use the word " Inspiration" in a
wide sense, from the plenary and infallible inspiration of Holy Scripture, down to the " holy inspiration whereby we think those things that be good ;"
they pray that in searching out the meaning of
Holy Scripture, God would " inspire" them with
the same Spirit, whereby that Scripture was
written ; but they do not use the terms " Scripture," &c. of any other books not in the primary
Canon, except the Apocrypha of the Old Testament.   One or two add some of the writings of the
corresponding period in the New Testament, the
Apostolic age, but the designation of the Apocrypha
as Scripture is universal.   And herein their practice
remarkably corresponds with that of our own
Church ; the mode in which our Homilies cite the
Apocrypha is in exact accordance with, and illustrates
the language of the Ancient Church ; both knew
that they were not, in the same sense, Scripture, as
the authoritative Hebrew Canon ; yet, as by both
they were publicly read in their worship, so both
cite them at times indiscriminately with the higher
Scriptures, and under the same titles ; believing
apparently that, even after the Spirit of prophecy

was suspended in its fulness and authoritativeness, during the intervening period before It again descended in Its fulness on our Lord, It still continued to guide the thoughts of some in a more authoritative way than was permitted to any after our Lord came, not as an independent revelation, but commenting on, developing, and applying, the meaning of the earlier, until the Sun of righteousness arose.

Article xix.

" The visible Church of Christ is a congregation of faithful men (cœtus fidelium), in the which the pure word of God is preached and the Sacraments be duly ministered, according to Christ's ordinance in all those things that of necessity are requisite for the same.

This Article seems to have been treated of, rather for completeness and for truth's sake, than for any immediate subject of controversy. For few would not now shrink from holding that all the Churches under the obedience and in the Communion of Rome were not in such sense true Churches, as to be a portion of the one Visible Church. Words nearly corresponding in the Confession of Augsburg are indeed in their " Apology for the Confession" so interpreted as to seem to deny to the Roman Churches the title of a Church ; for, while admitting that a society which holds the foundation, remains a Church, although it build

thereon hay, straw, stubble, it goes on to say[g],
" Most of those things which our adversaries
mention *overthrow the faith*, as that they condemn
the article of remission of sins, in which we say
that remission of sins is received by faith." Such,
however, (though the like sentiments may have
been and are still held by some in our Church,)
is not the current opinion of the Divines of our
Church ; nor though our reformers borrowed, with
some modifications, the language of the Confession
of Augsburg, can we be any way tied to Lutheran
expositions of it, which would be to acknowledge
them as authoritative documents in our Church.

With regard then to the Church of Rome, to
take such as rather lean to the opposite side, Bp.
Hall[h] adopts the

" charitable profession of the zealous Luther, ' We
profess that under the Papacy there is much Christian
good, yea, all, &c.   I say, moreover, that under the Papacy is true Christianity, yea the very kernel of Christianity, &c.' and that, on the very ground, that it held
the fundamental truth in the Creeds, ' Neither do we
censure that Church for what it hath not, but for what
it hath ; fundamental truth is like that Maronean wine,
which if it be mixed with twenty times so much water,
holds its strength ; the sepulchre of Christ was over-
whelmed by the Pagans with earth and rubbish,—yet still,
there was the sepulchre of Christ ; and it is a ruled case
of Papinian, that a sacred place loseth not the holiness
with the demolished walls ; no more doth the Roman lose

[g] Apol. p. 117. ed. Tittm.
[h] The Old Religion, c. 1.

the claim of a true visible Church by her manifold and deplorable corruptions; her unsoundness is not less apparent than her being; if she were once the spouse of Christ and her adulteries are known, yet the divorce is not sued out."

And Bp. Davenant[i], almost commenting on the notes of a Church mentioned in the Article, alleges both sufficiently to exist in the Romish Church;

" For the being of a Church does principally stand upon the gracious action of God, calling men out of darkness and death, unto the participation of light and life in Christ Jesus. So long as God continues this calling unto any people, though they (as much as in them lies) darken this light, and corrupt the means which should bring them to life and salvation in Christ; yet where God calls men unto the participation of life in Christ, by the word and by the Sacraments, there is the true being of a Christian Church, let men be never so false in their expositions of God's word, or never so untrusty in mingling their own traditions with God's ordinances. Thus the Church of the Jews lost not her being of a Church when she became an idolatrous Church. And thus under the government of the Scribes and Pharisees, who voided the commandments of God by their own traditions, there was yet standing a true Church, in which Zacharias, Elizabeth, the Virgin Mary, and our Saviour Himself was born, who were members of that Church, and yet participated not in the corruptions thereof. Thus to grant that the Roman was and is a true visible Church, (though in doctrine a false, and in practice an idolatrous Church,) is a true assertion, and of greater use and necessity in our controversy with Papists about the perpetuity of the Christian Church, than is understood by those that gainsay it."

---

[i] Letter to Bp. Hall appended to the Old Religion, t. ii. p. 77.

Amid this strong language as to the actual state of the Romish Church, Bp. Davenant holds that to be a " true Church," in which men may be saved, the " pure word of God" being, as Bp. Hall says, those " fundamentals of the faith," the doctrines of the Creed, into which we are baptized. It is indeed to be feared that the Romish Communion, as a whole, has, in the loss of the Cup, sustained a grievous privation ; but they who against the Churches in the Communion of Rome would on this ground press the words " duly ministered according to Christ's ordinance in all those things that of necessity are requisite to the same," should shew how (sad as the loss is) it is more essential, than the absence of consecration by a Minister, who through the Apostles has derived his commission from Christ.

The latter part of the Article (the omission of which has been animadverted on) states only, what all in our Church lament, that " the Church of Rome has erred in matters of faith" also ; it does not affirm it to have erred in such articles of faith as endanger salvation. Nor, again, has it appeared clear that our Article means more than to affirm that the Church of Rome, having erred, is consequently not infallible. It says not, in the present, " errs in matters of faith," but speaks in the past, " hath erred," just in the same way as it says of " the Churches of Jerusalem, Alexandria, and Antioch," that they " have erred," which was in time past.

A recent writer[k] says on this Article,

" The Article only affirms that the Roman Church has erred in matters of faith, e. g. in the case of Liberius and Honorius ; there is no assertion, that it does now err in faith. The object is to deny the infallibility of the particular Church of Rome."

At all events, it should ever be borne in mind, that the Church of Rome has, amid her corruptions, continued to be a faithful witness to the saving truths as to the Blessed Trinity, which were denied by the heretics of the early centuries, and which our Church, by retaining the Apostles' Creed as her summary of faith in her Baptismal Service and the Visitation of the Sick, acknowledges to be the substance of saving Faith.

Article xxi.

" General Councils may not be gathered together without the commandment and will of princes. And when they be gathered together, forasmuch as they be an assembly of men, whereof all be not governed with the Spirit and Word of God, they may err, and sometimes have erred, in things pertaining to God."

This being the only remaining Article on the Church considered in the Tract, we may as well take it now, although it relates only to a " private opinion" which the Author wishes to be regarded as admissible. It is, that there are certain Coun-

[k] Palmer on the Church, p. i. c. xi. §. 8. t. i. p. 316.

cils, viz. Œcumenical, which are not liable to err, and that the Article meant to take the term " General" in a popular sense, not denoting Councils strictly Œcumenical, but, as it is commonly used, Councils composed of Bishops from different Provinces, as opposed to " Provincial" or " National." And this last is plainly the meaning of the Article; for in that it says, not only that " General Councils *may* err," but that they " sometimes have erred," it does not mean to include Œcumenical Councils, since our Church receives the six Œcumenical Councils[1], and our best Divines speak of there having been six[m] or four[n] Œcumenical Councils *only*, according as they include the fifth and sixth in the third or fourth to which they were supplementary, or no.

[1] See Authorities, " Letter to the Bp. of Oxford," p. 44.

[m] The Homilies speak of " those[1] six Councils, which were allowed and received by all men," and of the last of the " four first General Councils[2]" as giving instruction even for matter of practice.

[n] Hooker, v. liv. 10. ed. Keb. Hammond on Heresie, sect. vii. and ix. expressly including the fifth and sixth. (In sect. 15. he says, " the first four or, if you will, six, or indeed any of the Œcumenical Councils truly so called.") Bp. Andrews defends K. James naming four (ad Card. Bell. resp. c. i. p. 20. c. vii. p. 160, 1.) in the latter place he accepts the sixth when it agrees with the four first, [i. e. excluding the spurious Acta,] but thinks the fifth and sixth *may* have been inferior.

[1] Against Peril of Idolatry, Part II. p. 190. ed. Oxf. 1822.
[2] On Fasting, Part I. p. 262.

Thus Field°:

" Concerning the General Councils of this sort, that hitherto have been holden, we confess that in respect of the matter about which they were called, so nearly and essentially concerning the life and soul of the Christian Faith, and in respect of the manner and form of their proceeding, and the evidence of proof brought in them, they are, and ever were, expressly to be believed by all such as perfectly understand the meaning of their determination. And that therefore it is not to be marvelled at, if Gregory profess, that he ' honoureth the first four Councils as the four Gospels ;' and that whosoever believeth them not, though he seem to be ' a stone elect and precious,' yet he lieth beside the foundation and out of the building. Of this sort there are only six ; the first defining the Son of God to be co-essential, co-eternal, and co-equal with the Father. The second defining that the Holy Ghost is truly God, co-essential, co-eternal, and co-equal with the Father and the Son. The third, the Unity of Christ's Person. The fourth, the distinction and diversity of His Natures, in and after the Personal Union. The fifth, condemning some remains of Nestorianism ; more fully explaining things stumbled at in the Council of Chalcedon, and accusing the heresy of Origen and his followers touching the temporal punishments of Devils and wicked cast-aways; and the sixth, defining and clearing the distinction of Operations, Actions, Powers, and Wills in Christ according to the diversity of His Natures. These were all the lawful General Councils (lawful I say both in their beginning, and proceeding, and continuance) that were ever holden in the Christian Church, touching matters of faith."

Œcumenical Councils then are very limited in number, and different in kind from mere General

° Of the Church, v. 51.

Councils; they are Councils of the whole Church, *which have been subsequently received by the whole Church;* and of these there are but six; the seventh General Council which is received by the Greeks, (the Deutero-Nicene Council,) was formally rejected at the time in the Western Church[p]; the several General Councils received by the Churches of the Roman obedience, are not received by the Greek Church, or by ourselves. Romanist theologians, on the contrary, as Bellarmine (whose definition of a General Council is " one[q], in which the Bishops of the whole Church may and ought to be present, unless they be lawfully hindered, and in which no one rightly presides except the Pope or one in his name," and who holds it to be " matter of faith that General Councils, confirmed by the Pope, cannot err either in faith or morals[r],") count, in

[p] The second Council of Nice was not at first recognized universally even in those Churches in which it was received, the Eastern and Rome. Only six General Councils are spoken of in the East, nearly 600 years after; (A. D. 1339,) by Pope Nicolas, a century after it, (A. D. 859,) and by Pope Adrian. (A. D. 871.) It was rejected by 300 Bishops of Gaul, Aquitain, Germany, and Italy, at the Council of Frankfort, (A. D. 794.) and called " a pseudo-synod" by Gallican and German writers from the ninth to the thirteenth centuries. Its degree of reception was owing to its being interpolated in the Liber Diurnus by Gratian, and then inserted in the Canon law; but the Council of Frankfort which rejected it, was never rescinded. See further, and authorities, in Palmer on the Church, p. iv. c. 10. sect. iv. add Perceval on the Roman Schism, p. 73 sqq.

[q] De Conc. i. 4.

[r] Ib. ii. 1.

all, eighteen such ; "other Romanist theologians contend for nine or ten, others for various larger numbers ; those who follow Bossuet agree in principle with ourselves, that the subsequent acceptance of a General Council by the universal Church alone makes it Œcumenical [*]."

Thus then there is ample scope for our Article in asserting, that "General Councils may err, and sometimes have erred," without touching upon Œcumenical [†]. The framers of our Articles were not here concerned with abstract propositions, but with matters of fact ; it was not their object to settle whether there were or were not certain Councils, which God might hereafter protect from error, as He had hitherto ;—such, namely, as have been received by the Church universal—but, both in defence and warning, to maintain that "General Councils" had in themselves no binding authority, nor were infallible. Were they so, our Church would of course be in error, in that she has pronounced contrary to Councils which the Roman Church counts general ; the Article was also a pro-

[*] Palmer on the Church, iv. 7.

[†] "The Article speaketh of General Councils indefinitely, without precisely determining which are General, which not, what is a General Council, what not ; and so may and doth include reputed or pretended General Councils, univocè general, though not exactly and truly indeed, (such as was the Council of Ariminum,) whereof I did not so much as intend to speak, my speech being limited with true and lawful, of which sort are not many to be found." Bp. Montague, Appeal, p. 125.

test beforehand against any thing which might be enacted against the truth she maintained, by any Council such as could then be brought together, and claiming to itself the title of " General," as did the Council of Trent : it remains a valuable warning to all Councils beforehand, before God has set His seal upon them.   As in the case of individuals, so it may be with the Church.   We know that there are individuals, who will finally persevere ; but who they are is not known even by themselves, unless God specially reveal it to them ; and this knowledge when He vouchsafes, He has probably always given, as to Daniel and St. Paul, towards the close of life.   Earlier, He gives hopes, earnests, dim intimations, to His faithful ones, and to most, probably, according to their faithfulness ; but it seems from His dealings, as though the certain assurance that any one would be saved, were too much for an individual during " the burthen and heat of the day."   In like way, it might be injurious for any number of individuals, such even as a General Council, to know beforehand that they would be infallibly guided into truth ; it might lead to presumption, might weaken that sense of dependence, humility, the diligent preparation and watchfulness, and the earnestness of the prayers, upon which their inerrancy depends ; and yet as there are some such Councils which God has preserved from error, so there may be a certain class, which it has been ever His purpose, secret to themselves, so to preserve ; and we may hope that should He allow any Council hereafter, like the six Œcumenical, to receive the sanction of the Universal Church, He will preserve this also from error. Certainly, this case is not liable to the risk of presumption which attends the theory of infallibility prevalent in the Romish Church, since, whether the Council is Œcumenical or no, is known by the event, depending upon its *subsequent* reception by the universal Church[u]. And again, since our Lord's promise is to the whole Church, but no General Council hitherto has, or probably could, in itself[x], at the time of its assembling, fully represent the Universal Church, but would probably consist of the *minority* of her Bishops, who might be misled, and might be disowned by the

[u] Hammond on Heresy, sect. xiv. rests the " inerrableness of General Councils," chiefly on their " finding approbation and reception among all those Bishops and Doctors of the Church diffused, which were out of the Council," since this makes it the act of the whole Church. In this the more moderate Theologians in the Romish Communion agree with him. (Palmer on the Church, p. iv. c. 7. p. 151.)

[x] Hammond, ib. sect. vi. §. 7. 8. 15. " For that any Council of Bishops, the most numerous that ever was in the world, (much less a but major part of those few, that be there present,) is not yet really the Universality of Christians, is too evident to be doubted of. It can only then be pretended, that it is the Universal Representative, or such an assembly, wherein is contained the virtues and influences of the whole Universal Church. And thus indeed I suppose it to be, as often as the doctrines there established by universal consent (founded in Scripture and tradition), have either been before discussed and resolved in each provincial Council, which have sent their delegates thither from

Churches which they professed to represent, it would follow that no General Council could claim to itself the guiding Presence of its Lord, with the same confidence as we may trust that it is pledged to the Church Universal. Certainly, there would be something so shocking in the thought that the whole Church should accept an erroneous decision in a matter of the Faith, that one should think it would be a relief to any one, not to think himself obliged to aver, (as a thing certainly determined,) that Councils, in such sort Œcumenical, " may err." But, in truth, I feel convinced that, as such Councils were not in the minds of the framers of the Articles, so neither were they contemplated by such as objected to the interpretation given, and that this objection will be readily dismissed. Hammond certainly sets it down, without offence, as a pious opinion, that Œcumenical Councils would not err [z].

all the parts of the world, or else have Post-factum, after the promulgation, *been accepted by them* and acknowledged to agree with that faith which they had originally received. When a doctrine is conciliarly agreed on, it is then promulgated to all, and the Universal, though but tacit, approbation and reception thereof, the no considerable contradiction given to it in the Church, is a competent evidence, that this is the judgment and concordant tradition of the whole Church, though no such resolution of provincial Synods have preceded."

[z] Of Heresie, sect. ix. " Of such [Councils truly General] none yet ever erred, that ever I yet read or observed, in points fundamental, and therefore I saw and see no cause but a man may say, such a Council shall never err in fundamentals." Bp. Montague, Appeal, p. 123. add, more at length, sect. 14.

" Though I make it no matter of faith, because delivered neither by Scripture nor Apostolical tradition, yet I shall number it among the ' Piè credibilia,' that no General Council, truly such, 1. duly assembled, 2. freely celebrated, and 3. universally received, either hath erred, or ever shall err, in matters of faith."

I may add in illustration, that some of our own Divines[a] instance the Council of Ariminum as a General Council which erred, although in the end confirmed by the Pope Liberius, but not universally received. And herein some of the Divines in the Romish Communion agree.

" Thus[b] Waldensis expressly affirmeth, that ' General Councils have erred and may err, and confidently delivereth, that it is no particular Church that hath assurance of holding the truth and not erring from the faith, neither that of Africa, which Donatus so much admired, nor the particular Church of Rome, but the Universal Church; nor that Universal Church which is gathered together in a General Council, which we have found to have erred sometimes, (as that at Ariminum under Taurus the Governor, and that at Constantinople under Justinian the younger in the time of Sergius the Pope, according to Bede and certain others,) but that Catholic Church of Christ, which hath been dispersed throughout the whole world, by the ministry of the Apostles, and others their successors, ever since the Baptism of Christ, and continued unto these times, which undoubtedly keepeth the true faith and the faithful testimony of Christ, teaching babes heavenly wisdom, and retaining the truth constantly in the midst of all extremities of errors.' "

[a] e. g. Field, v. 51. p. 664.
[b] Field, l. c. p. 663. see other opinions, ibid.

And in this, it should be observed, that there is a drawing near of Divines in the Romish Communion to the principles of our Church, not of ours to theirs; and on the ground which these take in common with ourselves, they might, if God hereafter should give them repentance, rescind the Council of Trent, as not being a Council truly General or Œcumenical, being neither free, nor adequately representing the whole Church, (but being rather an Italian Council,) nor having been subsequently received by the Church Catholic. But they approach to us, by abandoning what is Romish, and adhering to what is Catholic in their Church, and we maintain what is Catholic and approach not to what is Romish. For it is not the holding Œcumenical Councils not to have erred, or trusting assuredly that they never will err, which approximates to Romanism, but holding that General Councils (be the Bishops present exceeding few, as the non-Italian Bishops at the Council of Trent) are Œcumenical and authoritative, if confirmed by the Pope. Rather the Romanists, in so far as they are such, disparage even Œcumenical Councils, in order to make room for the authority of the Pope. As Field says [c],

" And therefore howsoever we dare not pronounce that lawful General Councils are far from danger of erring, (as some among our adversaries do,) yet do we more honour and esteem and more fully admit all the General Councils,

* l. c. 31. 51. fin.

that ever hitherto have been holden, than they do, who fear not to charge some of the chiefest of them with error, as both the second and the fourth for equalling the Bishop of Constantinople with the Bishop of Rome, which I think they suppose to have been an error of faith."

And this then may serve as an instance how an approximation between us and certain Divines of the Romish Communion does not necessarily imply any advances on our part to Romanism, and may open a prospect (however faint and distant it may now be) how, without the sacrifice of any truth, the Church may, on the principles of our own, again, if God vouchsafe, become one.

Article xxv.

" These five, commonly called Sacraments, that is to say, Confirmation, Penance, Orders, Matrimony, Extreme Unction, are not to be counted for Sacraments of the Gospel, being such as have grown, partly of the corrupt following (pravâ imitatione) of the Apostles, partly from states of life allowed in the Scriptures ; but yet have not like nature of sacraments (sacramentorum eandem rationem) with Baptism and the Lord's Supper, for that they have not any visible sign or ceremony ordained by God."

On the same ground, that our Church did not contradict itself, it is plain that the exposition given of this Article in the Tract is the correct one, that

" this Article does not deny the five rites in question to be [in some sense] sacraments, but to be Sacraments in the sense in which Baptism and the Lord's Supper are Sacraments ; (Sacraments of the Gospel) sacraments with an outward sign ordained of God."

D

For since the Homilies call marriage a " Sacrament[h]," it follows that the Articles do not reject
the five rites as being in *any* sense " Sacraments."
They neither restrain " Sacramental rites" to these
five, nor deny that these five may in some larger
sense be Sacraments.   There is also a remarkable
correspondence between the Articles and the Homilies, in that both use qualifying and guarded
expressions in speaking of the title of these rites
to be called " Sacraments."   Our Articles do not
introduce words at random.   It has then some
meaning when our Articles say, they " are not
to be counted for *Sacraments of the Gospel*," that
they " have not *like* nature of Sacraments ;" or the
Homilies " that in the *exact signification of a Sacrament* there be but two," or that " Absolution is *no
such Sacrament* as Baptism and the Lord's Supper
are," or that " neither it *nor any other Sacrament*
else be *such* Sacraments as Baptism and the Communion are," or that " the ancient writers in giving
the name not only to these five, but also to divers
other ceremonies, did not mean to repute them as
Sacraments *in the same signification* as the two ;" or
that " S. Augustine, in the *exact meaning* of the
word, makes mention expressly of two."   And
with this coincides the definition of our Catechism,
that there are " two only, generally [i. e. univer-
sally] necessary to salvation," the others so entitled,
not being of universal obligation, but relating to

[h] Sermon on Swearing. Part I.

certain conditions and circumstances of life only. Certainly persons, who denied these rites to be in any way Sacraments, (according to those larger definitions of S. Augustine, "a sacred sign[i]" or "a sign[k] applied to things of God," or of the Schoolmen[l] "a sign of a sacred thing,") would have said so at once, and not have so uniformly and guardedly said on each occasion, that they were not such, in the "*exact*" or "the *same* signification," the "*exact*" meaning," "*such*," "of the *like* nature;" nor, of one which they regarded as in no sense a Sacrament, would they have said "neither it, nor any other Sacrament else."

Nor is this, as I have elsewhere[m] pointed out, any approximation to the Romish view of the seven Sacraments; since 1) (which is of most moment) the Romanists studiously confound the difference between the two great Sacraments, which derive into us the very life of our Lord, and the other rites, which may be, and some certainly are, (if faithfully received) means of grace, "but are not, (to use our friend's words[n] of the two great Sacraments) "*justifying* rites, or instruments of communicating the Atonement, which is the one thing

[i] De Civ. D. x. 33.
[k] De Doctr. Christ. iii. 6. quoted by Bp. Jewel, Answ. to Hard. p. 82.
[l] P. Lombard, l. iv. dist. 1. ib.
[m] Letter to the Bp. of Oxford, p. 106 sqq.
[n] Newman on Justification, lect. 6. v. fin.

necessary to us ;" 2) our Church does not, as he also observes, " strictly determine the number."

This view of the relation of these five rites to the two great Sacraments, was clearly stated, without offence, by the sound and judicious Thorndike[o].

" That which remaineth for this place is, the consideration of the nature and number of the Sacraments, which being essentially ceremonies of God's service, the right resolution of the controversy concerning it must needs consist in distinguishing the grounds upon which, and the intents to which they are instituted; the difference whereof must make some properly Sacraments, the rest, either no Sacraments at all, or in a several sense and so to a several purpose. And truly, of all the controversies which the Reformation hath occasioned, I see not less reason for either side to stand upon their terms, than in this; which stands upon the term of a Sacrament, being not found in the Scriptures attributed either to seven or to two. For being taken up by the Church, that is to say, by those writers whom the Church alloweth and honoureth, what reason can deny the Church liberty to attribute it to any thing, which the power given the Church enableth it to appoint and to use, for the obtaining God's blessing upon Christians ? Why should not any action appointed by the Church to obtain God's sanctifying grace, by virtue of any promise which the Gospel containeth, be counted a Sacrament ? At least, supposing it to consist in a ceremony, fit to signify the blessing which it pretendeth to procure. For it is manifest, that Baptism also, and the Eucharist, are ceremonies signifying visibly that invisible grace, wherewith God sanctifieth Christians. But there will be therefore no

[o] Epilogue, book iii. p. 342.

consequence, that Baptism and the Eucharist should be counted Sacraments for the same reason and in the same nature and kind, for which any thing else is or can be counted a Sacrament. No, not though they may all in their proper sense be truly called Sacraments of the Church, because the dispensing of them all is trusted with the Church.—These two Sacraments have the promise of grace absolutely so called, that is, of all the grace which the Gospel promiseth; which it is to be acknowledged and maintained, that no other of those actions, that are or may be called Sacraments of the Church, doth or can do, upon the like terms as they do."

The distinction which he lays down between the two great Sacraments and the five rites is, that

" These " two immediately bring forth God's grace, as instruments of His promise, by His appointment; the rest must obtain it by the means of God's Church, and the blessing annexed to communion with it."

" Upon these terms," he proceeds to shew that all the other five rites may, in their right use, " very well be counted Sacraments of the Church," and thus sums up [q],

" In fine, the name and notion of a Sacrament, as it hath been duly used by the Church and writers allowed by the Church, extendeth to all holy actions, done by virtue of the office which God hath trusted His Church with in hope of obtaining the grace which He promiseth. Baptism and the Eucharist are actions appointed by God, in certain creatures, utterly impertinent to the effect of

[p] ib. p. 344.　　　　　[q] ib. p. 349.

grace, setting aside His appointment; but apt to signify all the grace which the Gospel promiseth, by virtue of that correspondence which holds between things visible and sensible, and things intelligible and invisible: both, antecedent for their institution to the foundation of the Church; the society whereof subscribeth, upon condition of the first, and for communion in the second.   The rest are actions appointed to be solemnized in the Church by the Apostles, not always every where precisely with the same ceremonies, but such as always may reasonably serve to signify the graces, which it prays for, on the behalf of them who receive them; the hope of that Grace being grounded upon God's general promise of hearing the prayers of His Church which the constitution thereof involveth.   Nor am I solicitous to make that construction, which may satisfy the decrees of the Councils of Florence and Trent, who have first taken upon them to decree under Anathema, the conceits of the school in reducing them to the number of seven; but seeing the particulars so qualified by ancient writers in the Church, and the number agreed upon by the Greek Church as well as the Latin; I have acknowledged that sense of their sayings, which the primitive order of the Catholic Church enforceth.   For though I count it a great abuse to maintain simple Christians in an opinion, that the outward works of them, not supposing the ground upon which, the intent to which, the disposition with which, they are done, secures the salvation of them to whom they are ministered, which opinion the formal ministering of them seemeth to maintain, yet is it a far greater abuse, to place the reformation of the Church in abolishing the solemnities rather than in reducing the right understanding of the ground and intent of those offices, which they serve to solemnize.

You will well know that neither in this, nor in any thing else which I may allege, do I wish to assimilate our language to that of the Church of Rome, or even to use that of our Homilies, when they call Marriage a " Sacrament :" it would be unnatural and affected and worse ; I would (since in these days one must speak of self, and may more naturally in writing to a friend) rather use the language of the fathers as to other things than to these, lest I should seem to be speaking not in a Catholic but in a Romish sense ; yet one need do neither ; on the contrary, since the word " Sacrament" has been misused to place the five rites on a level with the two great Sacraments, and there is no necessity for retaining it, it were wrong and cruel to risk perplexing person's minds by reviving it ; the truth which our Homilies imply may also be conveyed in other ways': but in truth it is not our language, but our feelings towards holy rites, which we need to have altered ; and I feel assured that a more reverend estimation and a more hallowed use of these gifts of the Church, as means whereby grace is bestowed, or enlarged. or restored, so far from placing them on a level with the two high Sacraments, would the rather raise men's veneration for these, as being so far above them. Men's real objection to considering these rites as in any degree " Sacramental," arises, it is to be feared, partly in their low estimate of

---

᷄ e. g. Mysteries, sacramentals, see Hooker, E. P. iv. 1. 2. ed. Keble. Beza calls the imposition of hands, " this as it were sacrament." Ib.

God's gifts thereby, or of the sanctity required of
the confirmed, the married, the Priesthood, or of
the grievous hindrance which sin interposes to the
shining in of Christ's light and grace upon the soul,
which Absolution tends to remove, but partly also
in their inadequate thought of the two great Sacraments.   When these, instead of being instruments
of knitting the soul to Christ, are regarded, in the
ordinary sense, as " means of grace" only, i. e.
aids to spiritual improvement, there is no room
for inferior sacramental actions.   But if we regard
these as instruments of conveying grace, and yet
the two Sacraments as so removed above them, as
to be instruments of a different kind, then will these
the rather take the place which our Lord gave
them in the Christian life, as the appointed chan-
nels for applying the Atonement to the soul, the
communication of Himself and His life.   On the
other hand, it would tend indefinitely to raise the
whole tone of our life and conversation, were we,
after the manner of the fathers, to look on holy
actions as having in them something sacramental,
as being, although inferior to the great Sacraments,
employed, in a mysterious way, to convey His
grace to us, and so as being mysteries; if we
habitually regarded institutions, some of which
are even now accounted " means of grace," as being
such, in that (whereby alone they could be such) God
gives them power, which of themselves they could
not have, and endows them with heavenly virtue;

if we looked on God's part in them rather than
our own ; if we regarded " preaching" such, because He puts His words into our mouths, and
" sends His blessing, that His word spoken by our
mouths, may have such success that it be not
spoken in vain';" or, with those of old, accounted
" fasting" sacramental', because, as our Homily"
says, " fasting used with prayer is of great efficacy
and weigheth much with God," and " obtaineth
notable things at His hand ;" and our Lord says,
" This kind goeth not out but by prayer and fasting";" or the " Creed'," because its recital is not
only a confession of our faith and a praise of God,
but because He makes it a means of deepening in
us the faith which we profess; or " prayer'," because
it is the voice of God within us to Himself ; or our
" Lord's prayer," because it hath " such wealth of

* Prayer in Ordination of Priests.
' Sacramentum Esuritionis, S. Hilary, ap. Jewel Defence of
the Apology, p. 215.
* On Fasting, Part II. p. 272.
* Matt. xvii. 21. quoted ib. in proof of the efficacy of fasting.
* " Receiving the Sacrament of the Gospel Creed, inspired by
the Lord, instituted by the Apostles, of which the words are few,
the mysteries great," Liturgy of Gelasius ap. Ass. cod. lit. i. 11.
so also the old Gothic and Gallican (ib. 30.) speaks of " the
Sacrament (or mysterious meaning) of the whole Creed." In
the Old Gallican (ib. 41.) the Creed is called " the seal of the
Catholic Faith, the Sacrament of eternal life." Much of the
language is from S. Augustine, who also (Serm. 228 fin.) speaks
of the " Sacrament of the Creed, which they ought to believe,
the Sacrament of the Lord's prayer, how they ought to ask."
* S. Hilary in S. Matt. c. 5.

spiritual virtue," we " offer to God of His own, and the Father recognizes the Son's own words[a];" or " Holy Scripture[b]," because it has a Divine power placed within it, as the word emanating from the Word ; or " Martyrdom[c]," because it is a renewal of Baptism, being a sharing of the Baptism, wherewith our Lord was baptized.

And, while this would be beneficial to ourselves and no approximation to any error, it could not fail to attract the respect of our brethren in the Romish Communion, when they saw that we denied to these rites the name and character of true Sacraments of Christ, not as undervaluing them as His gifts through His Church, nor from an irreverent habit of mind, but rather from exceeding reverence for those two,—one of which, Holy Baptism, it is the tendency of their own system to lower, but—which are the special witnesses of His Presence in the Church, the pledges of His love, engrafting and cementing the members of His Church into Himself, and deriving His life into them ; those two which issued from His pierced Side, in the hour when our Redemption was completed.

Article xxviii.

" Transubstantiation, or the change of the substance of bread and wine, in the Supper of the Lord, cannot be

[a] S. Cyprian de Orat. Dom. §. 5. and 1. he speaks §. 5. of the " Sacraments of the Lord's prayer." See also S. Aug. note y.

[b] S. Hil. ap. Jewel, l. c.

[c] S. Jerome Ep. 69. ad Ocean. quoted ib.

proved by Holy Writ; but is repugnant to the plain words of Scripture, overthroweth the nature of a Sacrament, and hath given occasion to many superstitions."

A right notion of what is meant by Transubstantiation is of the more importance to us, because there is no more common hindrance to the reception of the true doctrine of the Holy Eucharist, than the confused ideas prevalent about it. Nothing is more common than for any high statements of that doctrine to be attacked under the name of Transubstantiation or Consubstantiation. Persons acknowledge in act, (there is reason to trust,) what they dare not realize in words. They rightly dread the gross and carnal doctrine, rejected by our Church as Transubstantiation; they rightly shrink from that of Consubstantiation, as being an approach to it; and more justly might they reject both doctrines as novel, unauthorized, and rationalizing ways of explaining the *mode* of Divine mysteries; " how these things can be." But not having any clear notions what is meant by these statements, they dread to acknowledge any spiritual unseen presence of that blessed Body and Blood, and thus incur the risk of losing much of the awe with which those holy Mysteries should be approached and received, the belief of the actualness of their own union with Christ, the reality of their being temples of the Holy Ghost, and their own consequent consecration, and the comforts which they might also have in the belief of this union of earth and Heaven, of their real incorporation in the mystical Body of their Lord, and their receiving in themselves the pledge of their Resurrection, the earnest of their acceptance at the Day of Judgment. Not knowing what Presence it is which is implied in the doctrine of Transubstantiation, as defined in the Roman schools, and popularly received, they shrink from holding any actual Presence at all, other than in the believer's soul, which they dimly apprehend; not knowing what change is implied by Transubstantiation, they dread to avow that there is any change at all, but look on the consecrated elements, as remaining *simply* what they were before, and what to sight they seem. This is a very serious practical evil; and I have stated but the least portion of it; for it is doubtless one concurrent cause why many, it is to be feared, think of the Holy Eucharist solely as a commemorative rite, approach it and depart from it carelessly, or are lukewarm about it, and neglect it altogether. The infrequency of our Communions has been abated, the devoutness of Communicants (as you will yourself have observed in this place among others) has much increased, in proportion as the higher doctrines have been received.

In opposition then to these vague apprehensions, our friend has stated what the doctrine of Transubstantiation opposed in the Articles is;

" The shocking doctrine, that ' the Body of Christ,' as the Article goes on to express it, is not ' given, taken, and taken after an heavenly and spiritual manner, but is carnally pressed with the teeth;' that it is a body or substance of a certain extension and bulk in space, and a certain figure and the due disposition of parts, whereas we hold that the only substance such, is the bread which we see."

And a little afterwards[d], in summing up,

"We see then, that, by Transubstantiation, our Article does not confine itself to any abstract theory, nor aim at any definition of the word substance, nor in rejecting it, rejects a word, nor in denying a ' mutatio panis et vini,' is denying every kind of change, but opposes itself to a certain plain and unambiguous statement, not of this or that Council, but one generally received or taught both in the schools and in the multitude, that the material elements are changed into an earthly, fleshly, and organized[e] body, extended in size, distinct in its parts, which is there where the outward appearances of bread and wine are, and only does not meet the senses, nor even that always. Objections against ' substance,' ' nature,' ' change,' ' accidents,' or the like, seem, more or less, questions of words, and inadequate expressions of the great offence which we find in the received Roman views of this sacred doctrine."

[d] p. 51.

[e] e. g. Bonaventura in answer to the question, " Whether the Body of Christ is on the Altar in its own natural dimensions" (quantitas) argues, " The Body of Christ is living; and if living, organic; and if organic, hath dimensions (si organicum, quantum), therefore if on the Altar it be not detached from life, neither is it from dimensions," also " The Body of Christ or Christ sees them and hears, although It speaks not, lest It be discovered, but the outward senses presuppose dimensions; therefore it is there in dimension." L. iv. dist. 10. art. i. q. 2.

One may add, that the same appears from the very words of the Article itself, for it is this carnal doctrine alone which " is repugnant to the plain words of Scripture," (in that S. Paul speaks of that received by Communicants as " bread," 1 Cor. x. 17. xi. 27, 28.) it also " overthroweth the nature of a Sacrament," as being " an outward visible sign of an inward spiritual grace," whereas on this theory of Transubstantiation what we see would not be a sign but the reality.

The same view of the Article, that it is " not *any* change which is meant," is given by Bishop Jewel ;

" We affirm that the bread and wine are the holy and heavenly mysteries of the Body and Blood of Christ, and that by them Christ Himself, being the true Bread of eternal life, is so presently given unto us, as that by faith we verily received His Body and Blood. Yet say we not this so as though we thought, that the nature and substance of the bread and wine is clearly changed and goeth to nothing."

Or to take the statement of a modern Romanist [b], commenting on the articles of Trent,

" The bread and wine after consecration are in the eyes of faith nothing else than the Body and Blood of Jesus Christ, not that the bread and wine are annihilated, but because faith thenceforth contemplates there nothing but the Presence of Jesus Christ. This is the sense in which the ancients spoke of a change, but this is not that of the

[b] Courayer on P. Sarpi Hist. du Conc. du Trente, l. iv. t. i. p. 623.

Council, which teaches that the *whole substance of bread and wine is annihilated,* and that there remains nothing but the accidents and appearances.   *This* was *then the received doctrine of the Roman schools,* although even to the present day many of their theologians give this opinion only as one simply probable."

The more common statement among the School-men, and in Bellarmine[c], differs in words only,

" The bread is in truth not annihilated, *although nothing-remains of it after the consecration.*"

It is intended only to convey the same doctrine with more philosophical accuracy, inasmuch as " annihilation" implies " not merely[d] that nothing remains of a thing, but that it passeth into nothing," " but the elements are not supposed to be reduced to nothing, but to be changed as to their entire substance," " into a better substance," i. e. the Body and Blood of Christ. The other mode of speaking, however, also occurred[e].

This, and no other, is the doctrine of Transubstantiation opposed by our Articles and our great writers ; they confess fully the reality of Christ's Presence in the Sacrament, they only do not define the mode of His Presence ; they will not so tie down the Omnipotence of Almighty God that the Bread and Wine should not also be the Body

[c] De Euch. iii. 18.
[d] Bonav. l. iv. dist. xi. q. 3.   " What is changed into any thing is not annihilated."   Thom. Aq. l. iv. Hist. xi. q. 1. art. 2.
[e] It is mentioned by P. Lombard, l. iv. dist. xi. art. 2.

and Blood of Christ; they agree with Catholic antiquity that there is a change, but only not such a change, whereby (in Bishop Jewel's words) "the nature and substance of bread and wine goeth to nothing." This is the received doctrine in the Romish Church, though happily (one must in candour add) not so defined in the Council of Trent.

I need not, for your information, set down any of these passages; this contrast runs through all our writers; a real change, as I said, they gladly accept; a true, real, substantial, Sacramental, Presence of our Lord and His Flesh, the Very Flesh which was born of the Virgin Mary, and is now glorified at God's right hand, they reverently confess; they only confess not, that carnal, scholastic theory which would explain away the Mystery, that the Elements, although the Body and Blood of Christ, are also Bread and Wine. They confess the truth; the mode of its being they leave, like the mystery of the Incarnation whence it is derived, undefined because incomprehensible by man.

Thus, to take some, for the most part already collected to our hands.

Bishop Ridley [*].

"Both you and I agree in this; that *in the Sacrament* is the very, true, and natural, Body and Blood of Christ;

[*] Fox, Acts and Mon. p. 1598, quoted by Laud against Fisher, §. 35.

even that which was born of the Virgin Mary; which ascended into heaven; which sits on the right hand of God the Father; which shall come from thence to judge the quick and the dead; only we differ *in modo*, in the way and manner of being. We confess all one thing to be in the Sacrament, and dissent in the manner of being there. I confess Christ's natural Body to be in the Sacrament by spirit and grace, &c. You make a grosser kind of being, inclosing a natural Body under the shape and form of Bread and Wine."

And Bishop Andrews [f].

"The Cardinal is not, unless ' willingly, ignorant,' that Christ hath said, ' This is My Body,' not ' This is not My Body *in this mode.*' Now about the object we are both agreed; all the controversy is about the *mode.* The ' This is,' we firmly believe; that ' it is in this mode' (the bread, namely, being transubstantiated into the Body), or of the mode whereby it is wrought that ' it is,' whether *in,* or *with,* or *under,* or *transubstantiated,* there is not a word in the Gospel. And because not a word is there, we rightly detach it from being a matter of faith; we may place it amongst the decrees of the schools, not among the articles of faith. What Durandus is reported to have said of old, (Neand. Synop. Chron. p. 203.) we approve of. ' We hear the word, feel the effect, know not the manner, believe the Presence.' The Presence, I say, we believe, and that no less true than yourselves. Of the mode of the Presence, we define nothing rashly, nor, I add, do we curiously enquire; no more than how the Blood of Christ cleanseth us in our Baptism; no more than how in the Incarnation of Christ the human nature is united into the same Person with the Divine. We rank it among Mysteries, (and indeed the Eucharist itself is a

[f] Answer to Bellarmine, c. i. p. 11.

E

mystery,) ' that which remaineth, ought to be burnt with fire,' (Ex. xii. 13.) that is, as the Fathers elegantly express it, to be adored by faith, not examined by reason."

And Bishop Montague [s], (alleging Bishop Bilson,)

" The disagreement is only in de modo præsentiæ, the thing is yielded to on either side, that there is in the holy Eucharist a real Presence. ' God forbid,' saith Bishop Bilson, ' we should deny that the Flesh and Blood of Christ are truly present and truly received of the faithful at the Lord's table. It is the doctrine that we teach others, and comfort ourselves withal." (p. 779 of the subject.)

And again [h],

" Be contented with, that it is " The Body of Christ," and do not seek and define how it is so, and we shall not contest nor contend, which God forbid the Church of England should maintain, said Bishop Bilson."

Bishop Forbes [i].

" The doctrine of those Protestants and others seems most safe and true, who are of opinion, nay, most firmly believe, that the Body and Blood of Christ is truly, *really*, and *substantially* present in the Eucharist, and received, but in a manner incomprehensible in respect of human reason and ineffable, known to God alone, and not revealed to us in the Scriptures, not corporal, yet neither in the mind alone, or through faith alone, but in another way, known, as was said, to God alone, and to be left to His Omnipotence."

[s] Appeal, c. 30. init. p. 289.
[h] ib. fin. p. 297.
[i] Consid. Modestæ, De Euchar. l. i. c. i. §. 7.

Archbishop Laud [k].

" His Altar, as the greatest place of God's residence upon earth, (I say the greatest,) yea, greater than the pulpit. For there 'tis ' Hoc est Corpus Meum,' ' This is My Body.' But in the pulpit 'tis at most, ' Hoc est verbum Meum,' ' This is My word.' And a greater reverence (no doubt) is due to the Body than to the word of our Lord. And so in relation, answerably to the throne, where His Body is usually present, than to the seat where His word useth to be proclaimed."

Bp. Taylor again fully admits, that the terms " real," " substantial," and even " corporeal," Presence might have a sound sense, if this last be understood as opposed to " figurative" or " in type ;" and that the very words of the article of Trent, " the Saviour is sacramentally present with us in His Substance,"

" if [l] they might be understood in the sense, in which the Protestants use them, that is, really, truly, without fiction or the help of fancy, but " in rei veritate" so as Philo calls spiritual things, ἀναγκαιόταται οὐσίαι, ' most necessary, useful, and material substances,' might become an instrument of united confession."

Nor does he hesitate to acknowledge what some, accustomed to the modern generalizing way of speaking, would at once identify with Transubstantiation, that by the " real Presence" is meant the

[k] Speech in the Star Chamber 1637, p. 47.
[l] Of the Real Presence of Christ in the Holy Sacrament init.

Presence of that very Body which our Blessed
Saviour took of the Virgin Mary.

" It is enquired[m], whether when we say, we believe
Christ's Body to be ' really' in the Sacrament, we mean
' that Body, that Flesh, that was born of the Virgin
Mary,' that was crucified, dead, and buried.   I answer,
I know none else that He had or hath, there is but one
Body of Christ natural and glorified ; but he that says,
that Body is glorified, which was crucified, says, it is the
same Body, but not after the same manner : and so it is
in the Sacrament, We eat and drink the Body and Blood
of Christ, that was broken and poured forth : for there
is no other Body, no other Blood of Christ : but though
it is the same we eat and drink, yet it is in another
manner.   And therefore when any of the protestant
Divines or any of the Fathers deny that Body which was
born of the Virgin Mary, that was crucified, to be eaten
in the Sacrament, as Bertram, as St. Hierom, as Clemens
Alexandrinus expressly affirm, the meaning is easy ;   they
intend that it is not eaten in a natural sense."

I would add one more extract on the Presence
of Christ in the Holy Eucharist, both as containing
in itself several other testimonies, and as occurring
in a Charge[n], animadverting upon some of the
language used on other subjects in our Tracts.

" When any of us speak of this great mystery in terms
best suited to its spiritual nature ; when, for instance, we
speak of the real Presence of Christ's Body and Blood
in the Holy Eucharist, there is raised a cry, as if we were
symbolizing with the Church of Rome, and as if this

[m] V. ib. §. 8.
[n] Bishop of Exeter's Charge, p. 69—71.

Presence, because it is real, can be nothing else than the gross, carnal, corporeal, presence indicated in Transubstantiation. Now here, as with respect to Baptism, I will not argue the point, but will merely refer to the language of our Church in those authorized declarations of its doctrine to which we have assented, and in those formularies which we have both expressly approved and solemnly engaged to use.

" It is very true, that none of these declarations or formularies use the phrase ' real Presence ;' and therefore, if any should attempt to impose the use of that phrase as necessary, he would be justly open to censure for requiring what the Church does not require. But, on the other hand, if we adopt the phrase, as not only aptly expressing the doctrine of the Church, but also as commended to our use by the practice of the soundest Divines of the Church of England, in an age more distinguished for depth, as well as soundness, of Theology than the present—such as Abp. Bramhall[o], Sharp[p], and Wake[r], (all of whom do not only express their own judgment, but also are witnesses of the general judgment of the Church in, and before, their days ; ' No genuine son of the Church of England,' says Bramhall, ' did ever deny a true real Presence;') if, I say, we adopt the phrase, used by such men as these, and even by some of those, who at the Reformation sealed with their blood their testimony to the Truth against the doctrine of Rome, (I allude especially to Bishops Ridley and Latimer[s]—and even to Cranmer, who, when he avoided the phrase so abused by the Romanists, did yet employ equivalent

[o] Works, i. p. 15.

[p] Sermons, vol. vii. p. 368.

[r] Discourse on the Holy Eucharist, c. 2. " Of the real Presence acknowledged by the Church of England."

[s] Ridley in Fox, p. 61. Latimer ib. p. 65. Cranmer, Preface to book against Gardiner, &c.

words,) it will be sufficient for the justification both of
them and of us to shew, that the language of the Church
itself does in fact express the same thing though in different terms.   Still, I fully admit, that Christian discre-
tion would bid us forbear from the use of the phrase, if
the objection to it were founded on a sincere apprehension
of giving offence to tender consciences ;   and not, as there
is too much reason to believe, on an aversion to the great
truth which it is employed to express."

Again, Thorndike[t] thus speaks of the change
made by Consecration, only denying it to be *such*
a change as involves the abolition of the Elements.

" Upon these premises, I am content to go to issue as
concerning the sense of the Catholic Church in this point.
If it can any where be shewed, that the Church did ever
pray that the Flesh and Blood might be substituted instead
of the elements, under the accidents of them, then I am
content, that this be counted henceforth the Sacramental
presence of them in the Eucharist.   But if the Church
only pray that the Spirit of God, coming down upon the
elements, may make them the Body and Blood of Christ,
so that they which received them may be filled with the
grace of His Spirit ;   then is it not the sense of the
Catholic Church, that can oblige any man to believe the
abolishing of the elements, in their bodily substance ;
because, supposing that they remain, they may nevertheless become the instrument of God's Spirit to convey the
operation thereof to them that are disposed to receive it,
no otherwise than His Flesh and Blood conveyed the
efficacy thereof upon earth.   And that I suppose is
reason enough, to call it the Body and Blood of Christ
Sacramentally, that is to say, as in the Sacrament of the
Eucharist.   It is not here to be denied, that all Ecclesias-

[t] Epilogue iii. 4. p. 30.

tical writers do, with one mouth, bear witness to the Presence of the Body and Blood of Christ in the Eucharist. Neither will any one of them be found to ascribe it to any thing but the consecration, or that to any faith, but that, upon which the Church professeth to proceed to the celebrating of it. And upon this account, when they speak of the elements, supposing the consecration to have passed upon them, they always call them by the name not of their bodily substance, but of the Body and Blood of Christ which they are become."

And, after having shewn this in detail, he thus sums up the evidence" of the Fathers, in contradistinction to the modern view which would make the only Presence of Christ in the believer's soul, and that as resulting, not from the consecrating words, but from the believer's faith.

" I will go no further in rehearsing the texts of the Fathers, which are to be found in all books of controversies concerning this, for the examination of them requires a volume on purpose. It shall be enough, that they all acknowledge the elements to be changed, translated, and turned into the substance of Christ's Body and Blood ; though as in a Sacrament, that is, mystically : yet therefore by virtue of the consecration, not of his faith that receives."

He then establishes " on the other side[x] that this change is to be understood with that abatement, which the nature and substance of the elements requires, supposing it to remain the same as it was," shewing from the same authors[y], and from

* p. 31.   [x] p. 32, 3.   [y] p. 33, 4.

the Canon of the Mass, that they imply that " the heavenly grace hinders not, nor destroys the earthly nature," and thus concludes :

" And upon these premises, I conclude, that, as it is by no means to be denied that the elements are really changed, translated, turned, and converted into the Body and Blood of Christ ; (so that whoso receiveth them with a living faith, is spiritually nourished by the same, he that with a dead faith, is guilty of crucifying Christ ;) yet is not this change destructive of the bodily substance of the elements, but cumulative of them, with the spiritual grace of Christ's Body and Blood ; so that the Body and Blood of Christ in the Sacrament, turns to the nourishment of the body, whether the Body and Blood in the truth, turn to the nourishment and damnation of the soul."

Again, such writers as Bp. Cosins and the holy Bp. Ken, think it no contradiction to the words of our rubric that " the *natural* Body and Blood of our Saviour Christ are in heaven and not here," to affirm that " Christ's Flesh comes to us to be our food," that " Christ Who is in heaven, is also on the Altar," i. e. that He is there really, though not in a carnal manner.

Bp. Cosins[z].

" We confess with the Fathers, that the ' mode' is ineffable and unsearchable, that is, not to be enquired and searched into by reason, but to be believed by faith alone. For although it seems incredible, that in so great a distance of place, Christ's Flesh should come to us, to be

[z] Hist. Trans. c. 3. §. 3.

our food; yet we must remember, how much the power of the Holy Spirit is above our understanding, and how foolish it is to measure His immensity by our capacity. But what our understanding comprehends not, let faith conceive."

Bp. Ken[a].

" O God Incarnate, how Thou canst give us Thy Flesh to eat and Thy Blood to drink; how Thy Flesh is meat indeed; how Thou Who art in Heaven, art present on the Altar, I can by no means explain; but I firmly believe it all, because Thou hast said it, and I firmly rely on Thy love and on Thy omnipotence, to make good Thy word, though the manner of doing it I cannot comprehend."

Of course, great care and wisdom must be used by any in reclaiming a term, which, like that of the " real Presence," has acquired a sense very different from its original, lest they seem to be using it in a Romish, rather than in a Catholic, sense; and indeed, on this whole subject, great reverence is needed, that none take a sort of pleasure in reclaiming words, because the use of them is now unwonted; for myself, I have preferred keeping to the words of our formularies; they are so full of doctrine that one seems to need no more, and they come with authority; yet other turns of expression, such as are sanctioned by some of the great writers above quoted, that ' the Body and Blood of Christ are really present,' might often be adopted without offence, when the words ' real Presence'

[a] Exposition of Church Catechism, licensed 1685.

would, from long use, rather suggest to the mind the Romish *mode* of defining that Presence.   But, whether any use the term or no in ordinary instruction, it is very important to vindicate it in the abstract, and shew that our Church in excepting against Transubstántiation, objects only to the scholastic mode of explaining the great doctrine which she holds,—a true, ' real Presence.'

It will be familiar to you, that scarcely any argument is now more common among Romanist controversialists than one founded on the wrong use of this term ; they prove, at once, from Scripture, the doctrine of the " Real Presence," and then infer (as though involved in it) that of Transubstantiation[x], i. e. they affirm the truth, and then infer from it their own mode of defining that truth ; and whereas our writers above quoted affirm that the question between us relates not to the Presence, but to the *mode* of the Presence, these, having proved the Sacred Presence, assume the only point at issue, the *mode* of the Presence. And this is, on their part, not unnatural, as having,

---

[x] Dr. Wiseman, Lectures 1836, Lect. 14—16, entitled on " Transubstantiation."   In the Advertisement to vol. 2. it is said, " the tenth lecture was upon the Real Presence *or* Transubstantiation," as though they were altogether the same.   So also Dr. Butler's " Truths of the Catholic Religion," Lect 1—5. Bellarmine treats the two doctrines (as they are) as distinct ; the " Real Presence," de sacr. Euch. l. i. ii.   Transubstantiation or " the *mode* of the existence of the Body of the Lord in the Eucharist." 1. iii.

out of our Church, to do with those who deny any peculiar Presence of Christ in the Sacrament ; yet, on the other hand, will it tend to draw away from our Church those of affectionate minds and childlike belief, who, seeking a real, substantial, union with their Redeemer,—to be, by the communication of His Body and Blood " verily and indeed" to their souls, knit in one to Him, " be one with Him and He with them,"—are, through inadequate statements of the reality of this holy Mystery, taught to seek in the Romish Communion, what is stored up for them in our own. Such minds enter not into any of the difficulties of the Roman doctrine of Transubstantiation ; they acknowledge it, not in the sense of the Roman schools, but as implying the same real change which our own authors assert ; they acquiesce in it as a name, but believe, under that name, that doctrine only, for whose sake they received it, the real true unfigurative Presence of their Redeeming Lord.

Article xxxi.

" The sacrifices (sacrificia) of Masses in which it was commonly said that the priests did offer Christ for the quick and the dead, to have remission of pain or guilt, were blasphemous fables and dangerous deceits (perniciosæ imposturæ). "

In explanation of this Article, our friend contends, that by the " sacrifices of masses" is not meant " the sacrifice of the Mass ;" much less then the Primitive practice of commemorating the faithful departed at the Holy Eucharist, or the belief that they derived benefit thereby.   He says,

" Here the sacrifice of the Mass is not spoken of, in which the special question of doctrine would be introduced ; but the sacrifice of Masses, certain observances for the most part private and solitary, which the writers of the Articles saw before their eyes and knew to have been in force in time past, and which involved certain opinions and a certain teaching."

And this, one should think, was sufficiently clear, 1) from the language of the Article itself, for why should it be supposed that " the sacrifice*s* of Mass*es*" meant " the sacrifice in *the* Mass ?" 2) from the language of writers of the time, who by " Masses" always mean " private Masses*." 3) They were the " private Masses" alone, which were said for the sake of gain, or were a source of

* e. g. In Sir T. More's, Supplication of souls, they say, " we have been eased and holpen and relieved both by the priests' prayers, of good virtuous people, and especially by the daily masses and other ghostly suffrages of priests, religious, and folk of Holy Church ;" (quoted at length, Tract 81. p. 9.) add Cranmer, Defence of the Catholic Doctrine v. 16. (quoted ib. p. 11.) where he contrasts the " many masses every day," " the daily private masses," " the selling masses," with " the one common mass in a day," still existing in the Greek Church.

gain, which our Article condemns as " perniciosæ imposturæ." This he has sufficiently illustrated out of the Homilies, Bishop Bull, Burnet, and even the Council of Trent, or to add one passage only out of Bishop Jewel [b].

" Then ye began to tell the simple that it was sufficient for them to sit by ; that your mass was a propitiatory sacrifice for their sins ; that it was available unto them, ex opere operato, although they understood not what it meant : that you had power to apply it to quick and dead, and to whom ye listed ; and that the very hearing thereof, of itself was meritorious. Upon this foundation ye erected up your Chanteries, your Monasteries, your pardons, your supererogations, and I know not what. Thus was the Holy Communion quite forgotten. Thus were your Masses multiplied above number. Thus ye came by that ye would have called your old gold."

The very point objected to by Bp. Jewel throughout this Article is " the plurality of masses ;" the very form of Legacy was, that " masses" might be said for the soul of the departed, and these were private, special, masses (not the public service of the Mass) applied, as our Article says, to " quick and dead," or, as Bp. Jewel, " to whom ye listed." It was held in the Schools, that particular masses were more profitable to the souls in Purgatory than the mass. Bonaventura [c] says,

" Suffrages are to release from pain or guilt ; but it is

[b] Answer to Harding, Art. 13.   Plurality of Masses, Dis. 3.
[c] L. iv. ol. 45. art. 2. q. 3.

more to make satisfaction for the debt of many than of one, and satisfaction is made more easily for the debt of one than of many ; therefore two need more suffrages than one ; therefore, if they are divided between them, each has less ; therefore, it does not seem that it extends equally to all."

It was also held, that whereas the " suffrages[d] of the Church in common benefitted most, cæteris paribus, those who most deserved to be benefitted, those offered specially, benefitted those most for whom they were performed ;" and this they must hold, since, if their special masses did not most benefit those for whom they were offered, " the Church[d] which offered them did absurdly."

Of course, as far as the ordinary oblation of the mass was considered as relating to the same ends, the Romish doctrine would be condemned in it also; but there is this difference, that the erroneous doctrine was the sole foundation and groundwork of the particular masses, it was their whole substance ; as Bonaventura says, they had no other object or ground, than the belief, that the masses said specially for departed souls, benefitted them, (in the words of the Article,) " to have remission of pain or guilt ;" whereas, as no such end is expressed in the Canon of the Mass, so it is also an appendage only to its doctrine, engrafted in later times upon it. Thus, the special masses drew men's thoughts entirely to themselves ; what was

[d] Ib.

supposed to be effected by the public sacrifice of the mass for the relief of souls in Purgatory was general only ; no one could feel assured what share in the benefit his own friends had ; it would be (in the doctrine of the Schools) '' according to his deserts :'' the special '' masses,'' on the contrary, afforded a definite relief ; they had no other end in view than that of applying to the relief of the individuals the infinite merits of Christ ; they concentrated the benefits of the Meritorious Sacrifice of the Cross, which they were thought to renew, upon the '' remission of pain and guilt'' of a single soul. I cannot then but think that the writers of the Article had, as our friend says, the '' private, special, masses'' mainly in view, although including the '' public mass'' as far as in doctrine it agreed with them.

And this doctrine it is important for people to view distinctly, lest, taking the words in a vague way, they should involve Catholic truth in the Romish error against which our Article is directed. In this Article, then, the popular Romish doctrine is described as a whole, that in '' the sacrifices of masses'' as '' was commonly said,'' '' the priest did offer Christ for the quick and dead, to have remission of pain and guilt.'' This is condemned as a whole, and it is obviously no legitimate interpretation to omit a portion of this doctrine, and infer that the writers of the Article would have condemned the rest without it. The errors it presupposes are the Romish doctrines of Transubstantiation and Purgatory, which are condemned elsewhere separately, to which it here adds the "common" statement of the doctrine of the "sacrifices of masses," which readily follows upon Transubstantiation, the "repetition of the sacrifice of Christ." It presupposes that the departed for whom it was offered, were held to be in a state of "pain and guilt," to obtain remission of them by that offering, and that, not an oblation or sacrifice commemorative of the One Sacrifice, and thereby acceptable to God, but of Christ Himself. "Then if the Priest do offer the Sacrament, he doth offer indeed Christ Himself[b]." Any doctrine which does not involve these statements is not the doctrine condemned by the Articles. This Bishop Ridley himself might alone shew, for he states his objection to the Romish doctrine of the Sacrifice to be founded on the error of Transubstantiation. "Transubstantiation is the very foundation, whereon all their erroneous doctrine doth stand;" and "*This kind* of oblation [the Romish] standeth upon Transubstantiation his cousin-german, and they do both grow upon the same ground." And the celebrated dictum of Bishop Andrewes[c], which has passed almost into a proverbial statement of the principles of our

[b] Respons. ad Card. Bell. c. 8.
[c] Brief Declaration of the Lord's Supper, p. 6. 17. 16. quoted more at length, Tract 81. p. 10.

Church, is but a following out of this of Bishop
Ridley, " Do ye take away from the mass your
Transubstantiation, and we shall not long have
any question about the Sacrifice."   Bp. Jewel
also in like words[c], states this to be the only point
at issue.   " S. Cyprian saith, ' we offer our Lord's
cup mixed with wine.'   But he saith not as you
say, ' we offer up *the Son of God substantially
and really* unto the Father.'   Take away *only
this blasphemy* wherewith you have deceived the
world, and then talk of mingling the cup, and
of the Sacrifice whilst ye list."   They are not
the words then, " offer Christ," which are in themselves condemned, but the doctrine of a real sacrifice
of Christ Himself, distinct from the sacrifice of
the Cross ; the words may be found in Christian
Antiquity, but not in this meaning, whereas in
those later times it certainly was again and again
stated, that there was in the Holy Eucharist not
only a sacramental oblation of His sacrifice,
pleading Its merits, and so obtaining mercy from
God, but " a real and true sacrifice of the Son
of God[d]," by virtue of Transubstantiation ; " a
sacrifice," in the words of a recent apologist[e],
" truly real, because Jesus Christ is really therein

---

    [c] Defence of Apology, p. 2. c. 5. v. fin. p. 140.

    [d] See Courayer's comment on Bishop Jewel's objections to
Harding's statements of the doctrine, Defense de la Diss. sur la
validité des Ordin. Angl. iv. 6. quoted Tract 81, p. 44—46.

    [e] Dr. Butler, lect. 8. p. 228.

contained, and really in it, under the symbols of His Passion, offered up to His Eternal Father:" and it is used as an argument [f] of the infinite value of that Sacrifice, that " the thing offered is of infinite dignity, inasmuch as *whole* Christ is offered." It is the corporeal offering of the Son of God which alone is objected to. Again, the words " to have remission of pain and guilt" restrain the condemnation in the Article to the application of Masses to souls in Purgatory; " the Sacrifice [g] benefits also very much the faithful departed who are being purged in Purgatory, to the mitigation and payment of punishments. This is to be held as matter of faith, as is clear from the Council of Trent, cap. 22. can. 3."

It is only questioned in the Roman schools whether it confers this benefit by the very act of offering (ex opere operato) or by way of impetration;

" It benefits [h] in both ways, some deny that it doth by the mere act of offering, as Melch. Canus, Dom. Soto, for they say that this sacrifice has not an infallible effect, but ' if God so will.' Whence it appears, that it does not benefit ex opere operato, since the fruit of this is altogether infallible in one capable of it, who does not place any bar; but the contrary is more probable, as held by Ricardus, art. 6. P. Soto. Lect. 7. de Euch. D. Thom. P. iv. D. 45. q. 2. n. 3. ad 3." " It

[f] Less. de Purg. art. i. dub. 10.
[g] Less. ib. dub. 9.
[h] Ib.

confers[1] benefit ex opere operato, which mode all Doctors and the more recent who write against heresies admit." " It confers[k] ex opere operato remission of temporal punishment."

The very words " pain or guilt" (pœnæ vel culpæ) which the Article uses, are those employed by the Schoolmen, who lay down, that " the punishment of Purgatory can cleanse us from the guilt (culpa) of venial, and from the punishment (pœna) of mortal sin[1]." And this it is which even Cranmer objects to, the " propitiatory sacrifice of the priests in their masses, whereby they may remit sin and redeem souls out of purgatory [m]."

Such then being the limitations which the Article itself furnishes,—that the doctrine which it condemns is one which implies Transubstantiation, a repetition of the Sacrifice of the Cross, and the deliverance of souls from pain and guilt in Purgatory, it follows that no other doctrine of the Eucharistic sacrifice is contemplated by it. That solemn doctrine has been maintained by the chief Divines and Bishops of our Church ever since the Reformation as before it, only separate from the errors

[1] Ib. dub. 7.
[k] Ib. dub. 8.
[1] See Bonav. L. iv. dist. 21. q. 2. p. 1. art. 2. who quotes also Alex. Alen. 4. p. q. 13. memb. 3. art. 3. §. 5. Richard. 4. Sent. d. 21. art. 2. q. 1. Steph. Brulef. 4. Sent. d. 21. q. 3. Pet. de Tarent. ib. q. 1.
[m] Answer to Gardiner, b. v. f. 3. p. 544. see Tract 81, p. 48, 49.

formerly blended with it; the language in which they
have expressed it, has varied, as they have feared
that the one or the other expression might countenance errors held in the Church of Rome; but it
is clear, from the first, that what Cranmer and
Ridley meant to object to were the Romish errors,
not the truth; and as our position became more
defined, and there was less apprehension that such
errors should find place among our people, that
truth came to be more definitely and systematically
enounced.   Both these points have been recently
treated of, and the statements of our Divines given
at such length [n], that it is not necessary here to
speak further on the subject.   I will therefore
only select two specimens, one shewing that the
very words " propitiatory [o] and impetratory," as
applied to the Eucharistic Sacrifice in a sound

---

[n] Tract 81, " Testimony of writers of the later English
Church to the doctrine of the Eucharistic Sacrifice," and its
Preface.

[o] " Propitiatory" is, as Thorndike explains it, that which
" doth render God propitious;" it is thus used by a modern
Romanist also, " we say, the Mass" [the Holy Eucharist] " is a
propitiatory sacrifice, that is to say, a sacrifice that renders God
propitiatory to men." Dr. Butler's Lect. 8. p. 226.   Bp. Overall
adopts the word as occurring in the fathers, Tract 81, p. 73. and
others also.   In the same sense, Nelson prays " that I may so importunately plead the merit of it" [the full perfect oblation on the
Cross] "in this commemoration of that Sacrifice, as to *render* Thee
gracious and *propitious* to me, a miserable sinner." ib. p. 303.
Those who with Bp. Jewel (ib. p. 61.) and Bp. Hall, (ib. p.
107.) take " propitiatory" in the sense of " being" or " making
a propitiation," must reject it.

sense, are not objected to by approved Divines in our Church ; the other as a distinct and clear enunciation of the doctrine from one of her present Bishops.

The first are words of the learned Thorndike P.

" After the consecration is past, having shewed you, that St. Paul hath appointed, that, at the celebration of the Eucharist, prayers, supplications, and intercessions be made for all estates of the world and of the Church ; and that the Jews have no right to the Eucharist, (according to the Epistle to the Hebrews,) because, though Eucharistical, yet it is of that kind, the Blood whereof is offered to God within the veil, with prayers for all estates of the world, as Philo and Josephus inform us ; seeing the Apostle hath so plainly expounded us the accomplishment of that figure, in the offering of the Sacrifice of Christ upon the Cross to the Father in the highest heavens, to obtain the benefits of His Passion for us ; and that the Eucharist is nothing else but the representation here upon earth, of what is done there ; these things, I say, considered, necessarily it follows, that whoso believes, the prayers of the Church, made in our Lord's Name, do render God propitious to them for whom they are made, and obtain for them the benefits of Christ's Death, (which he that believes not is no Christian,) cannot question that those which are made by St. Paul's appointment, at the celebration of the Eucharist, offering up unto God the merits and sufferings of Christ there represented, must be peculiarly and especially effectual to the same purposes. And that the Eucharist may very properly be accounted a sacrifice propitiatory and impetratory both, in this regard ; because the offering of it up to God, with and by the same prayers, doth render God propitious, and obtain

P Epilogue iii. 5. p. 42. quoted Tract 81, p. 169.

at His hands the benefits of Christ's Death which it re-
presenteth ; there can be no cause to refuse, being
no more than the simplicity of plain Christianity enforceth."

I add the other statement the rather, as being so
concise and yet so full an exposition of the doctrine, withdrawing nothing of the truth, and yet
so conveying it, that none can think that it goes
beyond it.

" Not[p] only is the entrance into the Church by a visible
sign, but that body is visible also in the appointed means
of sustaining the new life, especially in that most sacred
and sublime mystery of our religion, the Sacrament of the
Lord's Supper, the commemorative Sacrifice of the Body
and Blood of Christ ; in which the action and suffering of
our great High Priest are represented and offered to God
on earth, as they are continually by the same High
Priest Himself in heaven ; the Church on earth doing,
after its manner, the same thing as its Head in heaven ;
Christ in heaven presenting the Sacrifice and applying it
to its purposed end, properly and gloriously ; the Church
on earth commemoratively and humbly, yet really and
effectually, by praying to God (with thanksgiving) in the
virtue and merit of that Sacrifice which it thus exhibits."

Article xxii.

" The Romish doctrine concerning purgatory, pardons
(de indulgentiis), worshipping (de veneratione) and adoration, as well of images as of relics, and also invocation
of Saints, is a fond thing (res est futilis) vainly (inaniter)
invented, and grounded upon no warranty of Scripture,
but rather repugnant (contradicit) to the word of God."

[p] Charge of the Bishop of Exeter, 1836, p. 43, 44.

In speaking of this Article, it is necessary to bear in mind, as our friend has said, that the question is, not what is allowable to be taught, not what it is expedient to practise, but what private opinions a person may or may not hold, consistently with the tenor of the Articles. We received our commission to teach in this our Church, wherein we were made members of Christ, through her Bishops ; as then we have ample scope for teaching, in what she holds and delivers out of or agreeable to Holy Scripture, so we have no commission to teach opinions, which she practically excludes. Even as to practices, which *are* Catholic [q], as prayers for departed saints, a Minister of our Church would, I think, do wrong to inculcate in his sermons, any thing for which his Church gives no countenance. Much more as to points, which, not being Catholic, have no authority from the Church, as the interpreter of Holy Scripture, any more than from the direct teaching of Scripture itself. Still more, again, as to any such points, which, not being Catholic, have also once degenerated into dangerous errors; their introduction would too pro-

---

[q] By " Catholic *practices*," I mean such as were universally received in the Church ; " the Catholic *Faith*" is that Faith which the Church taught universally out of the Holy Scripture, and which is embodied in the Creeds. The Catholic Faith is necessary to salvation, and nothing of it may be parted with; Catholic practice may be laid aside, (as in this case by our Church,) if there be any constraining cause ; though, of course, with reverence and circumspection.

bably favour the bringing back of those errors, which were once derived from them, and which yet exist. The likelihood of *any* purgatorial process after this life cannot be safely taught even by any who holds it, while the Romish doctrine of purgatory still exists ; apostrophes to saints to pray for us, if they hear us, which—detached as they were from regular devotion and sparingly as they occurred— we find without apprehension of injury in the mouths of holy men at the close of the fourth century, would countenance idolatry in this.   It would be trifling with the deposit of a pure faith which God has committed to our keeping, and tampering with the souls of our people whom we might be leading into sin, were any one to teach such points as these. Much more strongly may one say, should any in this place abstain from inculcating upon the minds of the young, what, as being young, they might probably exaggerate, and give an undue prominence to in their own minds. But of this, I may safely say, there has been no instance, nor is there any tendency to it.   People in this place are far too much impressed with their own responsibility, and feel too deeply how much is at issue at this great crisis, to lead the minds entrusted to them off to any such questions as these, so far removed, in any case, from the centre of Christian life and doctrine. But even apart from consequences, our office, as we have often repeated, is within our Church ; to develope, bring out, incul-

cate her teaching, not add to her of our own minds
what we have not received.

But, assuming this, the question which our
friend had in view was, as I said, not what a
Minister might do, but what is the meaning of the
Article.   And, here, it seems to me equally plain,
and it is almost a truism to state, that since the
Article definitely speaks of the " Romish doctrine"
on these points, it does not mean to condemn any
other.   What opinion any of the framers of the
Articles may have had as to any doctrine on these
points, *not Romish*, or whether they had formed to
themselves any definite view, is altogether beside
the question ; they were not drawing up a system
of faith, which should comprehend the whole compass of the subject on which they spoke, but
setting definite marks against certain corruptions
existing and maintained in their own times, and
before their eyes ; they were practically providing
against a certain existing practical evil ; they were
not concerned to trace the origin of existing corruptions, but to warn against them as they existed ;
every thing else lay beyond their horizon, and
they were not contemplating it ; it was not their
concern, whether such or such a doctrine, approximating in whatever degree to the Romish, were
found here and there in the early Church ; rather,
with their practical veneration for the first ages
of the Gospel, the writers of those times, when
they do touch upon any such points, point out

the difference sooner than the resemblance, rather shew that what is found in primitive Antiquity is not Romish, than seek to identify it with the form, into which, (if it were so,) it, in later ages, passed.

The very wording of the Article " Romish doctrine," or, as it before stood, " doctrine of the Schoolmen," shews what was in the mind of the writers ; had they meant to condemn every doctrine of " purgatory" or " invocation of saints," they would obviously not have restrained their censure by the insertion of the word " Romish." No one could seriously contend, that while they spoke against the " Romish" doctrine of purgatory, they meant to include any views held by the " Greeks," or the belief in any purgatorial process, distinct from the Romish, whether supposed to take place at the entrance of Paradise or at the Day of Judgment. So to interpret the articles would manifestly be a mere inference, founded on the supposed opinions of the writers, which, since they did not choose to express, we have no right to intrude upon their words. It were an arbitrary stretch of their meaning, opening the way to any other comments. And yet it would probably be found that the popular system of interpretation, which our friend opposed, did this ; and not only in points, in which no direct evil consequences would result, but where true doctrine would be affected.

I am not herein speaking of any thing in this

place, where a tone of more accurate thought pre-
vails, (as neither was our friend's Tract written for
persons here,) but of the vague way in which the
doctrines censured in this Article are popularly
misunderstood, and the injury to sound doctrine or
to habits of mind thence ensuing. Thus, one cannot
but know, that together with the " Romish doctrine
of pardons," persons are taught to shrink from the
whole subject of primitive discipline, as something in-
terfering between the soul and its Redeemer, instead
of being beneficial to it ; that they would regard
the recommendation of confession,—not as an essential to absolution, but as expedient and healthful,
yet with the view not merely of " obtaining ghostly
advice and comfort," but of taking shame before
men,—as something Popish ; or again they would at
once condemn all thought of penance and self-chas-
tisement for specific sins, as connected with the
Romish doctrine of " satisfaction ;" or they look
with suspicion on any statement, that the Absolution solemnly pronounced in Christ's Name,
" by His authority committed unto us," is not
merely a comfortable " declaration" of His mercies,
but may alter the state of the soul in God's sight ;
that it is not merely a relaxation of " ecclesiastical
censures," which we have not, but may tend to
" loose the bands of those sins, which by our frailty
we have committed," and remove the obstructions
which sin presents to the shining in of the grace
of Christ upon the soul. There is, as you are

aware, a large negative theory on these subjects
afloat, too little informed, to know what it appre-
hends, and so apprehending every thing ; morbidly
sensitive of any thing which it thinks may unduly
exalt the Priestly office, but careless as to securing
our individual humility and self-discipline ; condemning under names whose real meaning people
know not, doctrines and holy practices, whose
efficacy they have never tried ; anxious to secure
our irresponsibility to man, our freedom from
external control, the non-interference of man
between the soul and its Maker, but not anxious
how to secure our sense of responsibility to God,
our exemption from lawlessness, our attainment
of all those blessings, which God intended for us,
as ministered through man ; jealous against super-
stition, not against irreverence.   Thus, together
with the " Romish doctrine of pardons," the whole
subject of Absolution is often discarded ;   with
Purgatory, the intermediate state ;   with invocation
of Saints, the feeling of communion with them in
the one Church, of which they are the perfected
members ; with the veneration of relics, the feeling
that " precious in the sight of the Lord is the death
of His saints," and the belief in the miracles, which,
in some cases at least in the early Church, He
certainly wrought through them ; thus admitting in
fact the very principles of infidelity, and rejecting on
à priori notions what were after all the " mighty
works" of God's hand ; or together with the un-Ca-

tholic veneration of images, people reject as superstitious all outward reverence for holy things and
places; they regard the Altar, whence the holy
Mysteries of our Redemption are distributed, as no
ways distinguished above the rest of God's House,
nor that House itself as sanctified by the presence
of Angels and the unseen coming of our Lord.
The mere Protestant walks up and down with his
hat on, " on holy ground," listening to the solemn
tones of the organ at Haarlem.

It is then, practically also, of moment to distinguish what our Article does condemn as Romish,
lest we involve under it feelings, and doctrines, and
practices, which are primitive. It is of moment to
us practically, since it cannot be concealed that
many are deterred from practices, which, though
not essential, might still be a great safe-guard to
them, and are countenanced or (under certain circumstances) recommended by our Church, by the
fear of approximating to something corrupt in the
Romish system. Thus, one cannot doubt, that
the more frequent use of Confession to God's
Ministers, (which our Church recommends in certain cases as a preparation for the Holy Communion or for death,) would be a great relief to
persons' consciences, a great protection against the
corruptions which gradually steal over and steal
away the young, a great promoter of conscientious-
ness. One cannot doubt again, that the restoration " fourfold" of what has been wrongly gotten,

or liberal distribution to the poor, in token of sorrow for sin and love to Him Who we trust will remit it, (which our Church recommends by the example of Zacchæus,) or the acts of humiliation of which she speaks with regret in her service for Ash-Wednesday, would be very healthful to persons' souls, and not any way approximate to the abuses of the Romish Confessional or their system of penances.   And for our Church generally, it is notorious that this indiscriminate condemnation of what may be a means of holiness, together with what is unholy in the practical system of Rome, is one of the most dangerous allurements to persons to seek in the Romish Communion, what they might have found, without its corruptions, in our own.

But, beyond this, it is of course right, without any view to consequences at all, to adhere to the truth ; and so not to extend any condemnation in our Articles to points not contemplated in them, even though unauthorized, or, as the result may have shewn, dangerous.   We may not forfeit truth for expediency ; if then our Articles be not so rigid, as some on a cursory view might imagine, and so do not exclude things unadvisable, which some might wish had been peremptorily excluded, we must not seek protection against their introduction by extending the meaning of our Articles, but in some other way, and trust in God's good Providence for our safety, not look for it by maintaining an interpretation which, though convenient, is un-true. It does not follow, then, that because any may maintain a certain doctrine or practice not to be condemned by our Articles, he therefore thinks that it would not be very inexpedient or, under the circumstances, unlawful ; the use of the " ora pro nobis" (of which I shall have to speak presently) would probably in almost, if not all, cases, be so ; still, if the terms of our Articles do not pronounce upon it, we must be content to think that it is best thus, and seek for a remedy against any contingent risk in some other way.

To enter then a little into the details, which our friend, (as he has since stated,) omitted in the first instance to consider, lest he should seem to imply any definite practices to be allowable, which he only shewed our Articles not to disallow, the framers not seeing any necessity to pronounce upon them.

1. *Romish Doctrine of Purgatory.*

The chief characteristics of the Romish doctrine of Purgatory, seem to me, that it is 1) a *state* of suffering, 2) of punishment.

Thus to take the statement of two authors living among us, one[p] says,

" Catholics hold there is a Purgatory, that is to say, a place or state where souls departing this life with remission of their sins, as to the guilt or eternal pain, but yet liable to some temporal punishment (of which I have just

[p] Dr. Butler, lect. 6. on Purgatory.

spoken) still remaining due, or not perfectly freed from the blemish of some defects, which we call venial sins, are purged before their admittance into Heaven, where nothing that is defiled can enter."

Dr. Wiseman [q],

" From this subject of satisfaction, I naturally proceed to the consideration of another topic, intimately connected with it, the Catholic doctrine of Purgatory. The Catholic doctrine of satisfaction would be incomplete without it. The idea that God requires satisfaction, and will punish sin, would not go to its furthest and necessary consequence, if we did not believe that the sinner may be so punished in another world, as not to be wholly and eternally cast away from God."

In like way Bellarmine [r] says, the " true Catholic opinion" is that " Purgatory is only for those who die with venial faults, (1 Cor. iii.)—and again, for those who depart this life with punishment due (cum reatu pœnæ) their faults being already remitted."

These two statements seem to me its leading peculiarities; and, taken together, at once distinguish it from any thing found in the early Church. If any of the Fathers definitely hold that there will be suffering after this life, for some who shall be saved, it is not an abiding *state* of suffering ; and again it is spoken of, solely with respect to the future, the purifying for the Presence of the All-holy God, not as a

[q] Lect. II. on Satisfaction and Purgatory, p. 52.
[r] De Purg. ii. 1.

" satisfaction" for past sin, which " God requires."
These two combined points, then, sufficiently distinguish the Romish doctrine : add to this, that the
three Fathers of the African Church, who may be
thought most to approximate to the Romish doctrine, speak doubtingly; in the Romish Church it is
an article of Faith, so that Cardinal Bellarmine says[s],
that " whoso believeth not Purgatory, shall never
arrive thither, but be tormented with everlasting
burning in Hell."

It is, I should add, to me very questionable,
whether these very Fathers do hold a doctrine
bearing upon that of Rome : Tertullian[t] is
speaking of sufferings of the soul without the body
before the Day of Judgment, but has no hint that
they who so suffer, will then be saved ; rather he
implies that a portion of the sufferings is paid then,
without forestalling the full suffering, which is to
follow, of " soul and body in hell ;" and so the
text (Matt. v. 25. Luke xii. 58.) is understood by
S. Augustine in the same Church and by most
fathers[u], of being " cast into a prison" from which

[s] iv. dist. 21. quoted also by Bonaventura, &c.
[t] De Purg. i. 11.
[t] " In short, seeing we understand that prison, which the
Gospel points to, to be the ' place below' (inferos), and explain
the last farthing, of every slight sin for which, in the interval
before the resurrection, punishment is to be paid (luendum), no
one will doubt that the soul pays somewhat in the place below,
without forestalling the fulness of the resurrection through the
flesh also." de anim. fin.
[u] S. Ambrose in Luc. S. Hil. in Matt. S. Aug. de Serm.

G

they should never come forth ; as indeed who of men could " pay the very last farthing" due to God? (comp. Matt. xviii. 25, 34.) Again, even Romanist Theologians have thought that S. Cyprian [x] is speaking of sufferings in this life, and this, from the context, appears to me most probable. S. Augustine has distinct and opposite conjectures, evincing that he had not a definite *opinion* upon this subject ; and even when [y], in opposing those who thought that all sins, however grievous, of baptized Christians who remained in the unity of the Church, would be remitted through temporal fire, he admits it to be a question, whether there be not such a fire, whereby lighter sins would be cleansed, the whole context leads one to think that he is speaking of privation of bliss and mental pain not of corporeal suffering. For he had, before, been speaking of the pains which they endured through temporal *losses*, who, holding

Dom. in Monte, l. i. §. 30. Theoph. ad Luc. S. Jerome in Matt. implies the same. Stapleton Antid. Ev. says, that few Catholics interpret it of Purgatory.

[x] " It is one thing to stand for pardon, another to arrive safe at glory; one to be sent to prison, there to remain till the last farthing be paid; another to receive at once the reward of faith and virtue; one thing to be tormented for sin in long pain and so to be cleansed, and to be purged a long while in the fire, another to have washed away all sin in martyrdom ; one thing, in short, to wait for the Lord's sentence in the day of judgment, another at once to be crowned by Him." Ep. 55. ad Antonian.

[y] Lib. ad Dulcit. q. i. §. 6—13. see the context more fully, Tract 79. p. 41. where his other conjectures are also given.

" the foundation," " built thereon wood, hay, stubble," i. e. temporal enjoyments, which yet they did not prefer to the " foundation," Christ ; and that " through this pain of having to forego them they were saved as by fire." When then he goes on to say,

" Something of this sort, *it is not incredible*, may take place after this life also, and whether it be so, may be enquired, (whether it can be discovered or no ;) that some believers, through a certain purgatorial fire, as they have more or less loved perishing goods, shall more slowly or speedily attain salvation ;"

it seems to me certain, that he had in view a " pœna damni" only, corresponding to the sufferings from privation in this life of which he had just spoken ; as his very words too, " shall more slowly or speedily attain salvation," seem to indicate what that privation was, viz. of the bliss of the Beatific Vision, such as, in the intermediate state, is vouchsafed to the saved.

To return, however, to the " Romish Doctrine." The points, which I have selected as characteristic of it, would,—nakedly as I have stated them,—give a very inadequate notion of the doctrine of Purgatory, as it was taught at the time of our Reformation. To fill up this outline, we must go back to the " doctrine of the Schoolmen ¹," to which our Articles originally referred.

---

¹ It seems strange that Dr. Wiseman, in his Letter to Mr. Newman, should not have known what Mr. N. meant by a

P. Lombard then changes into certainty the conjecture* of S. Augustine ; and then he applies to the Roman *state* of suffering, words in which S. Augustine is speaking, according to the Greek view, of a fire at the Day of Judgment ‘.   However, on the supposed authority of S. Augustine, it became a received maxim in the Schools, that the " fire" of purgatory " is more grievous than any thing that a man can suffer in this

term used commonly among Romanist writers also, the " doctrine of the Schools," namely, the Schoolmen, whose sayings formed " the received doctrine of the day."   Dr. Wiseman's answer, appealing to what himself and other Divines *now* teach, is wholly beside the mark ; the whole Letter consequently but leads away from the point at issue.   One does not like to say what seems personal, but who will guarantee that Dr. Wiseman's teaching was accounted sound, or sufficiently " Roman ?" Report certainly said otherwise, and spoke of doubts and misgivings felt in the highest quarters.

* In Ps. 37. §. 3. S. Aug. here as elsewhere, begins by owning that what he is going to say is but conjecture, " Et forte," " And perhaps."

‘ See Tract 79, p. 40.   Bp. Montague (Answer to the late Gagger of Protestants, p. 288, 9.) points out the differences between S. Aug.'s view and the Roman ; 1) S. Aug. calls it an " amending fire," (emendatorius).   Romanists hold Purgatory to be penal only. 2) He places it at the Day of Judgment, when the Romish purgatory ceases.   3) Bp. M. quotes the " ordinary Gloss" as understanding S. Aug. of the Day of Judgment.   It may be added that S. Aug. expresses the Greek view, in a passage corresponding to this, in the same work on the Psalms, (in Ps. vi. §. 3.) as also in another, (in Ps. 103. Serm. 3. §. 5. see Tract 79, p. 40, 41.) whereas in this work he no where even conjectures that the Purgatorial fire will be lasting.

life ;" Aquinas [x], from Gregory the Great, affirms, that " the fire of purgatory and hell are the same," and also, from himself, as the only difference, " that the [y] damned, as being lower in merit, are to be ranked lower in place ;" that " the [z] punishment is two-fold, one, of the loss of the Divine Vision (pœna damni), the other of suffering (pœna sensus), in that they will be punished with corporeal fire, and in either, the least punishment of purgatory is greater than the greatest of this life." Bonaventura says, " the doctors of our time commonly hold [a]," (as he does himself,) " that the purgatorial fire is corporeal or material," and " though S. Augustine seemed to doubt herein, other doctors remove all doubt from us," and he argues, at length, against the notion of a spiritual purgatory.

In any case, the pains were held to differ only in

[x] ib. ii. 3. Præt.
[y] ib. v. ad 2.
[z] ib. i. ad 3.
[a] This is affirmed also by Alex. Alens. iv. P. q. 15. art. 2. §. 2. Agazel. lib. phys. v. 4. ap. Rich. de Med. Vill. " since the fire which afflicteth souls in purgatory is more active than our fire, which yet is most afflictive of all elements," add Rich. himself iv. dist. 20. art. 2. q. 1. In Bonav. there are further quoted, Brulefer ib. q. 4. and Pet. de Tarantas. (afterwards Pope Innocent V.) ib. q. 3. Thom. Arg. ib. q. 1. art. 3. Less (in Thom. de Purg. c. i. dub. 2.) says, " It is *certain* that in Purgatory there is punishment of suffering [not of privation only] ; that the punishment is by material fire is the common opinion of the Doctors, yet not matter of Faith."

duration from those of hell, (with regard to which the same question was raised whether the fire was material,) and hence it was argued that the fire was the same.

" Because[b] those souls suffer the same punishment as the damned, namely, the punishment of privation [of God's Presence] and suffering, and this differs only in that it is not eternal, as is the punishment of the damned, therefore it agreeth hereto, that they should suffer in the same place and by the same fire."

Bonaventura says further that souls remain there longer or shorter, as they remained longer or shorter in sin[c], and that

" The manifold authority of the saints establishes, that some, namely venial, sins may be remitted not in this world only, but also in purgatory, and since there is no room there for deserts or for sacraments, such punitive or purgatorial fire is called in aid, so called because the soul is purged from the dross of sin, and from venial faults, if it depart with them[d]."

Further, this state was considered capable of alle-

[b] Less. l. c.

[c] So also Alex. Alen. l. c. q. 3. In Bonaventura there are also quoted Richard. l. c. q. 2. Brulef. l. c. q. 5.

[d] " ' Final grace effaces venial sin in the act of the dissolution of soul and body,' &c. This was said by those of old, but now *it is commonly held* that venial sin, being taken hence by many, is purged in purgatory as to the guilt also." Albert. M. comp. Theol. verit. iii. 13. quoted by Abp. Ussher, " of purgatory:" add also Alex. Alens. l. 3. memb. 3. art. 3. §. 5. In Bonav. are also quoted Rich. l. c. q. 1. Brulef. l. c. q. 3. Pet. de Tarantas. l. c. q. 1.

viation through indulgences ; of which more presently. It is stated also as a probable opinion , that
individuals remained in purgatory during centuries.
Yet more, in order fully to realize what the writers
of our Articles had in view, in condemning the
" Roman doctrine" of purgatory, we ought to take
into account the popular tales and representations
circulated at that time, the pictures in which it was
exhibited, the vivid descriptions given of it, the detailed visions in which it was said to have been revealed ; the lengthened period of thousands of years,
during which it must be supposed to last, since the
indulgences remitted thousands of years of suffering.
And on this ground alone, it must practically have
effaced the thought of Hell in the minds of the
people, since so long temporal punishment will in
itself fill the mind, and leave no room for the thought
of any thing beyond it.

The above abstract statements, however, though
they give no idea of the *practical* character of the
doctrine, suffice to explain what the Article means
by the " Romish doctrine of Purgatory ;" according
to which it was " a lengthened *state* of actual suffering, as well as of privation of the Divine Vision,
without rest day or night, through real fire, and

Less ad S. Thomam de Purg. c. 2. dub. 4. " pains, which
else [i. e. unless daily masses were purchased], will hold them
here with us in fire and torments intolerable, only God knoweth
how long." Sir Thos. More, Supplication of Souls, Works,
p. 316.
" We—not yet importunately bereave you of your rest, with

that the fire of Hell, not only purifying the soul for the Divine Presence, but also satisfying the Divine Justice, exacting the punishment of sin, which, at departure from this life, remained unpaid, yet capable of mitigation through the treasure of merits at the disposal of the Pope."

Such then being the " Roman doctrine," it follows, of course, that a doctrine differing in kind from this, is not the doctrine contemplated, one way or other, in the Articles.   The supposition of a pœna damni, that those who were not " pure in heart" might not for a long period be admitted to " see God," and that this privation might itself be purifying ; that the whole period between the departure from the body and the Resurrection may be one of painless purifying of the soul, in order that it may be capable (in S. Irenæus' words) to " receive God ;" that persons may, by some sorts of sin, forfeit the fulness of the Presence of Christ in the intermediate state ; that, though with a cheering hope, they may not be certain of their salvation, any more than in this life they are ; and that under any of these circumstances, it may please God to give to such souls a larger portion of comfort and joy, through the prayers and oblations of the Church,—any of these suppositions are quite distinct from the Roman doctrine, which maintains " a temporary period of actual *suffering*."

crying at your ears, at unseasonable times, when ye would (*which we do never*) repose yourselves and take ease." Sir Thos. More, l. c. p. 288.   See, at length, Tract 81, p. 9.

On the other hand, the view found in Origen, S. Ambrose, S. Hilary, S. Jerome, S. Paulinus of Nola, S. Basil, and S. Gregory of Nazianzum, that " for[s] all but the highest saints in whom love dissolved all remaining dross whatsoever, some transient suffering, more or less in duration, was in store at the Day of Judgment," though it has the notion of " suffering," differs from the Romish, as to the time when it takes place, and that it is not a *state* of suffering ; nor again does it stand in any relation to the prayers of the Church. This view is accordingly condemned by Romanist writers as inadequate or erroneous[h], who thus again confirm the view, (if any such confirmation were needed,) that such is not the doctrine condemned by our Articles as the " Roman doctrine."

Our Article does not then condemn all notion of a purifying process after this life, but one distinct system ; and our Church has evidently taken the more humble line, not presuming to affirm or deny what has not been revealed, but denying the only view of Purgatory contrary to Holy Scripture, which for our consolation declares our departed to be at " rest," whereas this exhibits them in intense suffering. If any collect from the impression of Antiquity, a general awe of what may pass between death and Judgment, it may be that he will acquire more reverent thoughts of the exceed-

[s] Tract 79 on Purgatory, p. 35.
[h] Bellarm. de Purg. ii. 1. quoted Tract 79, p. 26.

ing holiness of God's Presence, and reflect more earnestly as to the fruits of actions or courses of action, and learn to speak less peremptorily, one way or the other, when Holy Scripture is silent ; but our Article leaves him free, so long as he maintain not that one doctrine which is " repugnant to the word of God."

In conclusion, since people are disposed to believe all things, which are said hardly of what they dislike, I may just observe, that neither in my own writings, nor in those of any of my friends, is there any trace of a tenet, which it has lately been affirmed [s] that we are " zealous in teaching," " that there is a Purgatory for the purification of the saints," nor do I hold it.   Our friend, as you know, has put it prominently forward as one of the chief points of our controversy with Rome [h].

2. *Romish Doctrine of Pardons.*

Our Article joins on the " Romish doctrine of Pardons" or " Indulgences" [indulgentiis] immediately to that of " Purgatory," thereby the more shewing what it was which it meant to condemn, the assumed power, namely, of the Pope to lessen by Indulgences the period of Purgatorial suffering.

[a] Edinburgh Review, No. 147. p. 272.
[h] Tract 79, and Lectures on Romanism.

This is illustrated by the citations of Bp. Jewel[i], shewing that " Pardons sprung out of Purgatory."

" Roffensis saith (contr. Lutherum. Polydor. de Inventor. l. 8. c. 1.) ' Thus Jansene : It cannot well appear from whom Pardons first began. Among the old Doctors and Fathers of the Church, there was either no talk at all, or very little talk of Purgatory. But as long as Purgatory was not cared for, there was no man that sought for Pardons. For the whole price of Pardons hangeth of Purgatory. Take away Purgatory, and what shall we need of Pardons ? Pardons began, when folk were a little feared with the pains of Purgatory."

" Johannes Major saith (in 4. Sent. Dist. 20. Quæst. 2.): ' Of Pardons little may be said of certainty : for the Scripture expressly saith nothing of them. Touching that Christ saith unto Peter, Unto thee will I give the keys, &c. we must understand this authority with a corn of salt,' (otherwise it may be unsavory.) ' Therefore certain' of the Pope's ' Pardons that promise twenty thousand years are foolish and superstitious [k].'

[i] Defence of Apol. c. 7. dis. 1. p. 486.

[k] The authenticity of these pardons has been disputed in modern times ; Bouvier, however, defends the principle on which they rest ; " it may happen that such indulgences would not be equal to a Plenary Indulgence. For let us suppose a sinner who [sin which] merited 10 years of Canonical penance ; let us also suppose a man who lived 20 or 30 years in the habit of frequently committing sin by thought, by desire, and by action, which is not uncommon ; in the language of the Prophet, he will have multiplied his sins beyond the hairs of his head ; each in particular will not merit less punishment than if it had been committed only once ; how great therefore would be the time of Canonical penance which this sinner should perform in order to comply with the Church discipline ? It is incalculable ; and even, in this case, it is probable it would be far from satisfying

" Your School Doctors themselves (Veselus) are wont sometime to say, ' The devising of Pardons is a godly guile, and a hurtless deceit; to the intent that by a devout kind of error the people may be drawne to godliness.'·

" Here Mr. Harding, you see the Antiquitie, Authoritie, and best countenance of your Pardons: that they flowed first out of the sinks of your Purgatory, as one vanity floweth out of another: you see that your Pardons some-times may be ' superstitious,' and full of ' folly:' you see that the sale of your Pardons is ' a godly guile,' and a devout kinde of error to lead the people."—

" Alphonsus de Castro saith (Lib. 8. Indulgentiæ): ' There is nothing that the Scriptures have less opened, or whereof the old learned Fathers have less written, than of Pardons. Of Pardons (in the Scriptures and Doctors) there is no mention.' "

God's justice, since we are ignorant of the proportion between the Canonical penance, and the diminution of the pains of the next life.   However, we hold that a Plenary Indulgence, per-fectly gained, would cancel this immense debt in all its extent! Therefore we ought not to condemn Partial Indulgences for being too long, provided they are well authenticated ; otherwise we should condemn Plenary Indulgences [1]."   In fact, also, the manifold Indulgences given to the members of religious frater-nities in the Romish Church would soon make up this sum. Thus to the members of the " pious sodality of the most sacred heart" of our Lord, indulgences are given annually of above 1600 years [1616 years and as many quarantines or periods of 40 days] besides 29 Plenary Indulgences ; to which are added 12 more, Plenary, for the daily recitation of the Rosary, besides other lesser ones, as 300 days for every contrite repetition of the Rosary, and 60 days for every good work devoutly performed. (" The pious sodality, &c. 8th edit. with the approbation of the most Rev. Dr. Murray, &c.")

[1] Taken from " A dogmatical and practical treatise on Indulgences," abridged from Bouvier's Work, Dublin, 1839.

Cardinal Fisher also says [1],

" It weighs perhaps with many, that we lay such stress upon Indulgences, which are apparently of but recent usage in the Church, not being found among Christians, till a very late date."

It is clear, then, from this, that nothing which existed in the Primitive Church was contemplated by our Articles, as of course the doctrine of Absolution could not be, which, in its strongest form, our Church recognizes in the " Order for the Visitation of the sick."   It condemns a doctrine, consequent upon the " Romish doctrine of Purgatory," and therefore, as well as that doctrine, unknown to the early centuries.   The " godly discipline" of the Primitive Church, our own, in her yearly humiliation, professes her desire to restore, though as yet unable.   But indeed the very term " pardons" or " indulgences" is notoriously a technical term for one specific doctrine connected with absolution, and does not relate to absolution itself, from which it is separated, as treated of by the Schoolmen.   Thus Thomas Aquinas gives us a summary of P. Lombard's teaching on this head[m];

" *After* the ' master' had laid down as to penance and the power of the ministry, to whom the dispensation of this sacrament belongs, he here lays down some things, which follow upon penance, in two parts.   In the first he lays

[1] Assert. Luth. conf. 18. quoted Tract 79, p. 50.
[m] In P. 4. dist. 20.

down the time of penance; in the second some things which
relate to the defect of penance.   The first falls into two
heads; it shews 1) that the time of penance is to the end
of life; 2) how they are to be dealt with, who repent at the
end; and this is two-fold.   He shews 1) how they who
repent at the end of life, obtain remission of sins, although
they are still debtors as to the temporal punishment,
which they will endure in purgatory after death; 2) that
the same punishment is owing to those, who in whatever
way do not complete worthy satisfaction in this life,
&c.'

Aquinas himself proposes his questions under
the following heads[1];

" 1) whether any one can by repentance at the end of
his life obtain pardon of sins; 2) whether the temporal
punishment, the charge whereof remains after penitence, be
estimated according to the amount of the fault; 3) whether
any of the punishment, whereby satisfaction is made, can
be remitted by indulgences; 4) whether any parochial
priest can give an indulgence; 5) whether an indulgence
avail to one in mortal sin."

" Indulgence" itself is thus defined[m]; " remission
of temporal punishment, due to God for actual sin,
given by the authority of the Church, exterior to
the Sacrament, by the application of those satis-
factions, which are laid up in the common treasure
of the Church."

And the " temporal punishment" so spoken of
not only includes the sufferings of Purgatory, but

[1] ib. q. 1. art. 1—5.
[m] Less. ad Thom. Aq. de Indulgent.

the chief character of Indulgences must necessarily be derived from it. The doctrine of Purgatory alone gives these their interest and importance. So long indeed as the shortening of the term of penance brought with it restoration to the communion of the Church, and in it to the participation of that Body and Blood, whereby we are cemented into the mystical Body of Christ, it was of course a great privilege ; such it was in the practice of the early Church on which Romanists profess their " indulgences" to be founded [n] ; the intercession of the martyrs, (although even it was abused [o] to " heal slightly" a grievous " wound,") in obtaining for the lapsed re-admission to the Holy Communion, did obtain for them inestimable privileges : again, an earlier reconciliation in the case of the dying was indeed a mercy, when in their extremities

---

[n] Dr. Wiseman, Lect. 12. on Indulgences, t. ii. p. 79. " The chief ground of indulgence or mitigation, and the one which most exactly includes all the principles of a modern indulgence, was the earliest, perhaps, admitted in the Church. When the martyrs, or those who were on the point of receiving the crown and had already attested their love of Christ by suffering, were confined in prison, those unfortunate Christians who had fallen [i. e. had abjured Christ under Heathen tortures] and were condemned to penance, had recourse to their mediation ; and upon returning to the pastors of the Church with a written recommendation to mercy from one of those chosen servants of God and witnesses of Christ, were received at once to reconciliation, and absolved from the remainder of their penance."

[o] S. Cyprian complains of the practice in most of his letters on " the lapsed."

and last conflict it obtained for them the restoration
of the " pledges of " their Saviour's " love,"
and placed them in Communion with Him : or,
again, when in the prospect of persecution, they
who had once denied the faith, were restored to
Communion, in the hope that they might overcome
wherein they had been overcome, this also was a
great privilege that they were not left to such a
conflict " unarmed, but were fortified with the protection of the Blood and the Body of Christ [p]."   But
when Communion came to be previously restored,
and Indulgences were only " relaxations of temporal
punishment," what great worth would they have,
if confined to this life ? Were they, as modern
Romanists exhibit them [q], only a mitigation of
penance enjoined by the Church, what great
interest would they have ? The wounded spirit
would rather dread them than long for them ; the
true penitent would rather dread to be released
entirely from the discipline and chastening, which
are the correction and remedy of his former sins ;
he takes cheerfully the chastenings of God's own
hand ; he accepts gladly the austerities or priva-

[p] S. Cyprian, Ep. 57. (Fell) mentions both these cases : Dr.
Wiseman, l. c. gives these as instances of early " indulgences."

[q] Thus Dr. Wiseman, l. c. drops all allusion to Purgatory.
Dr. Butler only alludes to any thing, *not* in this life, thus slightly ;
" this atonement, *if considered in this life,* consists either in the
penitential works prescribed in the canons, or imposed by the
confessor."   Lect. 5. " Objections against the several parts of
the Sacrament of Penance."

tions or self-denials, which may tend to deepen his repentance and approve its sincerity. To what end to be free from a wholesome though bitter medicine? The history of ascetics of all times shows, that earnest repentance craves no " indulgences;" men's own experience will tell them, that a discipline in conformity with their sin is joyous as well as healthful. But when the doctrine of " satisfaction," instead of being the expression and means of contrition, became the discharge of a definite debt to Almighty God, and this debt, if not discharged or released in this life, was thought to be still due after death, and paid by the sufferings of purging fire, and that, the fire of hell, though for a time only, then indeed any relaxation of the " temporal punishment" did acquire an exceeding value, not for the sake of any thing in this life, but to shorten those extreme and unknown sufferings, which were believed to be greater than any thing in this life ; which were intense as Hell ; from which there was no rest day nor night ; and to whose duration there was no certain limit, but the Day of Judgment. Any limitation of canonical penance shrinks into absolute insignificance, if not rather to be deprecated than to be purchased.

It is indeed remarkable, that Romanists admit that " Indulgences" do not supersede " penance," thereby shewing that " canonical penance," which they state to have been the object of that " mitigation which *most exactly* includes all the principles

H

of a modern indulgence*" is not the object of *their*
" indulgences ;" and they urge the continuance of
" penance," even after obtaining " indulgences,"
on the very ground that the real end of both is
not any thing in this life, but so to compensate
to Divine Justice that the penitents be not after
this life cast into Purgatory[b].   Purgatory then is
the real end of the modern system of " indulgences" and " penance :" of " penance," in the
Ancient Church, the end was, to escape Hell
by furthering such repentance as made the sinner
capable of God's mercies in Christ ;   the relaxations which Romanists parallel with their " indulgences," were restoration to the communion of the
Church.

[b] Dr. Wiseman, see p. 95. n. n.   " Indulgences of a hundred
years or more, if there are such, may be insufficient to compensate
the whole temporal punishment which a sinner is bound to pay . .
Hence, thirdly, sinners truly converted ought to endeavour daily
by good works [satisfactions] and indulgences, whether partial
or plenary, to diminish the debts which they owe to Divine
Justice and to compensate for them entirely in this life, lest
they be sent to the prisons of purgatory, and do not come out
thence till they have paid the last farthing."   Bouvier de Pœnit.
p. 301, quoted by Mr. Palmer, 3rd Letter to Dr. Wiseman, p. 7.
" We do not believe an indulgence to imply any exemption from
repentance . . . . . nor from the works of penance or other good
works, because our Church teaches, that ' the life of a Christian
ought to be a perpetual penance.' (Conc. Trid. de extr. Unct.)
No one can ever be sure that he has gained the entire benefit of
an indulgence, though he has performed all the conditions appointed for this end."   Dr. Milner End of Controversy, Lett. 42,
p. 304. 306. quoted ib.

" Pardons" then are altogether distinct from " pardon" through the power of the keys, because absolution relates to guilt, " pardons" to punishment ; absolution is spiritual, " pardons" outward only ; absolution, in whatever degree, alters a sinner's state towards God, " pardons" remit only a penalty due after restoration to God's favour ; absolution restores to Communion, and opens the soul to the grace of the Sacrament, " pardons" follow upon restoration ; absolution applies the power of the keys by virtue of Christ's authority committed to His ministers, " pardons," a certain treasure made up of the merits of Christ and of works of supererogation of His saints, supposed to be committed to the keeping of the Church ; absolution applies God's mercy through the Satisfaction of His Son, " pardons" relate to a " satisfaction" still due from man to God ; " pardons" are applied directly to the state of the soul after death, absolution only relates to it, in as far as it changes that state in this life ; " pardons" presuppose absolution, absolution does not involve any doctrine of " pardons." Their provinces, offices, ends, comforts, value, are not less distinct than their scripturalness and primitiveness, absolution being derived from the distinct promise of our Lord, as understood by the Primitive and Catholic Church, " pardons" are founded on a precarious extension of the fact, of which Scripture also gives instances, that God does not always, with the guilt, remit the punishment of sin, but which it neither declares to be His uniform rule, nor did His Church in her purer days believe that she had received from Him any influence in its suspension.   Rather, the infliction or continuance of punishment, even after aggravated sin has been repented of, seems to have so important a place in the Divine government, and (it may be) to be so connected with the Divine Attributes, as not to admit of any interference.   We see continually instances of it ; in many cases, it is annexed by a regular law, so that sin, persisted in to a certain point, entails punishment by a natural consequence, i. e. by certain effects resulting from the sin according to a fixed rule and brought about by it ; we do *not* see that when so annexed, it is ever remitted.   The very Intercession of our Lord, which obtains the restoration of the offender to God's favour, is not, as far as we see, applied to it.   It may be required, as I said, by the Moral Government of God or His Attributes, in some way we know not, that one who has sinned to a certain point, should remain under punishment in this life ; it *may be*, that it is essential to such continued penitence as may be necessary for him ; beyond this, we know nothing ; it is a fact which we see and know in God's dealings with men, not a truth of Revelation.   The Romanists have erred in assuming, 1) that it is uniform, 2) that it is a " satisfaction" to God's justice, 3) that it is a definite debt, which must be paid, and so if not paid in this life, is to be paid in Purgatory, 4) that the Church can interfere with it.

This, however, is the sole province of " Indulgences." They take up the offender, where absolution leaves him, and are a supplement to it. Absolution frees him from guilt, leaves him (according to Romanists) with a debt upon him to Almighty God. This debt it is the office of Indulgences to abate or extinguish.

The Schoolmen, accordingly, rightly deny that Indulgences are a mere relaxation of Ecclesiastical penance[o],—or that they depend " simply on the power of the keys, (in which case they could have been given by Priests,) whereas they require, over and above, jurisdiction and the power of dispensing the Church's treasure, which ordinarily belongs to Bishops alone, as being the husbands of the Church, and so having the disposal of that dowry which she had from her betrothing to Christ[p]." Again, it is distinctly stated[q], that they " release not from guilt (which is the power of the keys), but from punishment."

The connection of " Indulgences" with Purgatory, which Romanists among ourselves now suppress, is thus asserted by the Schoolmen.

" It[r] is most truly assumed, that the treasure of the

---

[o] Bonav. iv. Dist. 20. q. 2.

[p] ib. q. 3.

[q] ib. q. 4.

[r] Alex. Alens. 4. q. 24. Memb. 5. add Bonavent. iv. Dist. 20.

Church is in the power of the Pope, and that he can com-
municate its benefits to them, (since on account of the
charity wherein they departed they are fit objects to receive
the benefits of the Church,) and thus he can grant them
indulgences and relaxations."

" As by God' eternal punishment is changed into purgatorial, so by the priests purgatorial punishment into temporal."

" That' Indulgences profit the departed, who are de-
tained in Purgatory, if applied to them by the Church,
is certain, and the contrary is a heresy, or most close upon
a heresy."

Only the mode of application differs, it being
generally ruled, that since the departed are removed
out of the jurisdiction of the Church into that of
God, the Pope can no longer bestow these Indulgences as a judicial act, but only in the way of
obtaining the relaxation from God.

" The relaxation* may take place by the way of suffrage
or impetration, and not by that of judicial absolution or
commutation."

" Those* who are in Purgatory, Indulgences profit not
directly, yet indirectly they do profit them."

Even this, however, is matter of doubt among
them.   Ricardus de Media Villa, in citing a form of

c. 5. who quotes also S. Thom. Suppl. 3. p. q. 27. art. 1.
Brulef. iv. Dist. 20. q. 8. Pet. de Tarantas. ib. q. 22. Ric. de
Med. Villa, ib. art. 3. q. 3.
    * Al. Alens. ib. memb. 3.
    ' Less. in S. Thomam de Indulg. c. 5.
    " Alex. Alens. l. c.
    * Ric. de Med. Vill. l. c.

indulgence given for one departed, says, that this is the opinion of " some" only.

" Whoever[y] shall do this or that for himself or for his departed father, or for any other person, being in Purgatory, we give so many days' indulgence, but so, *according to some*, they do not profit them, except in the way of suffrage."

" It is the common opinion[a], that Indulgences are only bestowed by the way of compensation or of suffrage."

The extent to which they were carried is singularly illustrated by the question, discussed by the Schoolmen generally, " whether Indulgences avail as much as they promise"—so large were they, that it was argued, that " since merits were now so few, that a person could scarcely suffice for himself, the Church's treasure must have been long exhausted[a];" so vague, that they promised for the same act, (whether it cost much to the individual or no,) the same relaxation, as of " the third part of his penance[b]," whether it were ten or thirty years. Their moral effect is illustrated by the question, " whether if one in the prospect of the plenary remission of a jubilee committed more grievous

---

[y] l. c.

[a] Less. l. c.

[a] Bonav. iv. Dist. 20. q. 6. where there are quoted Alex. Alens. iv. p. q. 23. Memb. 2. S. Tho. in suppl. 3. p. q. 25. art. 1. Richard. iv. Sent. dist. 20. art. 3. q. 2. Brulef. ib. q. 9. Pet. de Tarant. ib. q. 22.

[b] Bonav. ib.

sin, (reserved cases) he would derive the benefits of it?" This is affirmed to be the most probable [c].

There is then ample proof that the doctrine and practice condemned in the Article is (as our friend stated) "not every doctrine about pardons, but a certain doctrine, the Romish doctrine, as indeed the plural form itself shews," and this as he further states, "the doctrine maintained and acted on in the Roman Church, that remission of the *penalties* of sin in the next life may be obtained by the power of the Pope, with such abuses as money payments consequent thereupon [d]."

3. *Invocation of Saints.*

The distinctions between the "Romish doctrine of Invocation of Saints" and any practice which may be found in the early Church, (although itself also not primitive or Catholic, but rather the vent of individual feeling,) have been so clearly and fully pointed out by an unsuspected authority, Archbishop Ussher, that one need but have referred to his work. It is one thing, however, to acknowledge a thing, another to have it vividly before our

---

[c] Less. ad Aq. cap. de Indulg. fin.

[d] This in Ed. 1. stood, "large and reckless indulgences from the penalties of sin obtained on money payments." In either case, the distinctive character of the doctrine was pointed out, an assumed release from the *penalties* of sin.

eyes ; and it is of so much moment to us on all sides, as well as to the Roman Church, to have a distinct perception of the difference between the early and the later practice, that I will set down the heads of Archbishop Ussher's contrasts, and at length subjoin the specimens which he gives of the later practice ; painful as is the exhibition of so much that is shocking in the devotions of a Christian Church. The differences then noted by Archbishop Ussher are these : 1) that in the Ancient Church, mental addresses were confined to God, as knowing the thoughts ; in the Romish, are made to the saints also. 2) In the Ancient Church, they spoke doubtfully, whether the Saints know the details of our wants ; in the Romish, it is held as a point of faith that they hear men's prayers. 3) In the Ancient, the Saints were applied to only in the same way as the living ; in the Romish, " formal and absolute prayers are tendered to them." 4) In the Ancient, they are addressed only as joint petitioners ; in the Romish, as advocates and mediators by virtue of their own merits also. 5) In the Ancient, the seeking the prayers of the Saints interfered not with our " boldness to approach the throne of grace ;" in the Romish, the Saints are held out as an easier and more acceptable way for a sinner to approach to God. 6) In the Ancient, persons were taught chiefly to look to their own prayers ; in the Romish, to the intercession of Saints.

7) " And principally," in the Ancient Church, the prayers of the Saints were requested as fellow-servants; in the Romish, " invocation is attributed as a part of the worship due to them, in Bellarmine's words ' an eminent kind of adoration.' "

These are mostly so many several ways of exhibiting how the ancient compellations of the Saints had no tendency to efface the thought of the " One God and the One Mediator between God and man," or to stop short in them ; which is miserably the tendency of much, encouraged by the Roman practice. In the Ancient Church, no service was asked of them, which might not be also rendered conjointly by our brethren on earth, nothing asked different in kind, nothing said which could even *seem* to centre in them ; they are not avenues of approaching to God, but, as part of the Church, joint intercessors with the members who are in the flesh ; nor, in asking their prayers, is *any office or service to them contemplated.* In forms, on the contrary, used in the Church of Rome, the Saints are (as far as the words go) ‘asked absolutely to render offices, which are in the power of God only ; if these prayers can be explained in any other sense, this is not their obvious meaning ; the words do not lead up to God, but in themselves rather lead away from Him, by resting in the creature ; they ask of St. Mary and of the Saints to " loose, heal, give life, &c." and do not suggest that they cannot do this by any power entrusted to them, much less by any virtue of their own ; the Saints are proposed for the time as the objects in which devotion is to centre ; and, if it be possible that some can use such prayers in a sound sense, still their tendency, and their actual effect upon the multitude, is to bind them down to the Saints, in whom the language terminates ; and this the more, since devotion to the Saints is on principle encouraged.

This last point, which Archbishop Ussher gives as a " principal" difference between the prayers of the Ancient and Romish Church, is of the more moment practically, because the same act will have a very different character, according to the frame of mind in which it is performed. Could Romanists shew ever so much (which they can not) that the direct forms " help me, heal me,") much less " do thou give heaven, remit sin,") were used in the Ancient Church, in insulated cases^c, this would

<hr/>

^c To take the only case in Antiquity of any account, (for the rest alleged by Dr. Wiseman in his recent " Remarks" are either spurious or nothing to the purpose,) the virgin Justina mentioned by S. Gregory. All which can be collected from it is, that having prayed at much length to The Father and our Lord, she in some way " besought the *Virgin* Mary to aid a *virgin* in danger :" we have not the words she used ; those of S. Gregory from the very antithesis are evidently oratorical ; they do not imply that she said in the modern Roman way " help me." She may only have asked her prayers ; this quite satisfies the language, and since we do not find the other form in those times, it is probable that she did no more. S. Gregory's relation is ; " Abandoning all other hope, she flees to God for refuge,

not bear out the modern Romish practice, in which
they are systematically a part of devotion. An
address to a saint, as the result of a momentary
feeling, is very different from habitual prayers to
them, *as devotion.* The one tends to substitute
them in the place of God, the other does not. The
one proposes them as an object of " worship, adoration," or whatever it may be called ; the other does
not. It matters not whether in the abstract it be
called latreia or douleia ; that which makes the
modern prayers to the Saints so sore an evil, is
that these prayers are recommended as devotion ;
the mind of the worshipper is directed to the Saints;
the prayers offered to them, in their obvious sense
terminate in them ; it must require a strong effort
of mind and much fixedness on God, to supply
another sense than what is the obvious meaning
of the words ; and few who have observed their
own habits of mind in prayer will think that such
forms as " do thou give heaven, do thou loose,
do thou heal, do thou remit sin, lead, conduct
thou to glory, preserve thou, help thou, take away
[sin], give life," addressed to a creature, are not

and takes as her defender, against that accursed passion, Him
to Whom she was betrothed." Then having given specimens of
her prayers to our Lord, he adds, " Having uttered these things,
and *much beside,* and beseeching the Virgin Mary to aid a
virgin in danger," &c. (τὴν παρθίνον Μαρίαν ἱκετεύουσα βοηθῆσαι
παρθίνῳ κινδυνευούσῃ.) S. Greg. Naz. Orat. 24. §. 10. 11. How
different this in tone from the sad extracts in Archbishop Ussher.
On other authorities quoted by Romanists, see below, p. 115. note.

a grievous snare, that they do not tempt people to idolatry, and must not, too probably, for the most part, end in it.

It is not our office to judge the Church of Rome, though it is an act of charity to her to warn her what a grievous scandal these things are, even in our eyes as men, and to remind her of the woe denounced on those "who offend one of these little ones who believe in" Christ, if so be she may have grace given her at last, herself formally to condemn what, although she has never formally sanctioned, yet still she has encouraged. Meanwhile for our immediate purpose, it appears from this, that there is a "Romish doctrine of Invocation of Saints" wholly distinct from any thing in the Church of the 4th Century, holding them out as mediators preferable to our Lord, commending devotion to them as a religious act, asking them not merely to "pray for us," but to give us what we pray for. There is then, on this ground, no reason to think that our Article in condemning "the Romish doctrine," or "the doctrine of the Schoolmen," on this point, had any reference to any thing found in the early Church, being wholly distinct from it. The painful evidence given by Archbishop Ussher of this sad declension of the Roman Church, is so detailed and so long, that it must be kept for another place[d].

This same distinction between the Romish Invocation of Saints and the earlier occasional addresses

---

[d] Note A. at the end.

to them is also thus clearly drawn out in a valuable and full statement by Thorndike*.

"I will distinguish three sorts of prayers to Saints, whether taught or allowed to be taught in the Church of Rome. The first is of those that are made to God, but to desire His blessings by and through the merits and intercession of His Saints. I cannot give so fit an example, as out of the Canon of the Mass, which all the Western Churches of that Communion do now use. There it is said, 'Communicating in and reverencing the memory of such and such of all Thy Saints, by whose merit and prayer grant that in all things we may be guarded by Thy protection and help.' There is also a short prayer for the Priest to say, when he comes to the altar, as he finds opportunity, 'We pray Thee, Lord, by the merits of the Saints, whose reliques are here, and all Saints; that thou wouldest vouchsafe to release me all my sins.' And on the first Sunday in Advent mentioning the Blessed Virgin, they pray, 'That we who believe her truly the Mother of God, may be helped by her intercession with Thee.'"

"The second is that which their Litanies contain.—The form of them is manifest, that whereas you have in them sometimes, 'Lord, have mercy upon us,' 'Christ, have mercy upon us,' 'Holy Trinity, One God, have mercy upon us;' you have much oftener the Blessed Virgin repeated again and again, under a number of her attributes; you have also all the Saints and Angels, or such as the present occasion pretends for the object of the devotion which a man tenders, named and spoken to, with, 'Ora pro nobis,' i. e. Pray for us. The Blessed Virgin some say with 'Te rogamus audi nos,' We beseech thee to hear us. One thing I must not forget to observe, that the prayers, which follow these Litanies, are almost

* Epilogue, b. iii. p. 356 sqq.

all of the first kind ; that is to say, addressed directly to
God, but mentioning the intercession of Saints or Angels
for the means to obtain our prayers at His hands.

" The third is when they desire immediately of them
the same blessings, spiritual and temporal, which all Christians desire of God.   There is a Psalter to be seen, with
the name of God changed every where into the name of
the Blessed Virgin.   There is a book of devotion in
French with this title ; ' Moyen de bien servir, prier, et
adorer la Vierge Marie,' The way well to serve, pray to,
and adore the Blessed Virgin.   There are divers forms of
prayer as well as private speeches, concerning her especially and other Saints, quoted in the Answer to the
Jesuit's Challenge, p. 303—345.   Of those then, the first
kind seem to me utterly agreeable with Christianity, im-
porting only the exercise of that Communion which all
members of God's Church hold with all members of it,
ordained by God, for the means to obtain for one another
the grace which the obedience of our Lord Jesus Christ
hath purchased for us without difference, whether dead or
alive ; because, we stand assured that they have the same
affection for us, dead or alive ; so far as they know us and
our estate, and are obliged to desire and esteem their prayers
for us, as for all the members of Christ's mystical body.
Neither is it in reason conceivable that all Christians from
the beginning should make them the occasion of their
devotions as I said, out of any consideration but this.
For, as concerning the term ' merit' perpetually frequent
in those prayers, it hath been always maintained by those of
the Reformation that it is not used by the Latin Fathers,
in any other sense than that which they allow.   Therefore
the Canon of the Mass and probably other prayers which
are still in use, being more ancient than the greatest part
of the Latin Fathers, there is no reason to make any difficulty of admitting it in that sense, the ground whereof I
have maintained in the second book.

" The third, taking them at the foot of the letter, and
valuing the intent of those that use them by nothing but
the words of them, are mere idolatries; as desiring of the
creature that which God only gives, which is the worship
of the creature for the Creator, ' God blessed for evermore.' And, were we bound to make the acts of them that
teach these prayers the acts of the Church, because it tolerates them and maintains them in it, instead of casting them
out, it would be hard to free that Church from idolatry;
which whoso admitteth, can by no means grant it to be a
Church, the being whereof supposeth the worship of One
God, exclusive to any thing else. But the words of them
are capable of the same limitation that I gave to the words
of our Lord when I said, that they whom Christians do
good to here, may be said to receive them into everlasting
habitations, because God does it in consideration of them,
and of the good done them. And so when Irenæus calls
the Virgin Mary the advocate of Eve, (v. 19.) he that
considers his words there and iii. 33. shall find that he
saith it, not because she prayed for him, but because she
believed the Angel's message, and submitted to God's will,
and so became the means of saving all, though by our
Lord Christ, Who pleadeth even for her as well as Eve.
Ground enough there is for such a construction; even
the belief of One God alone, that stands at the head of
our Creed, which we have no reason to think the Church
allows them secretly to renounce, whom she alloweth to
make these prayers. And therefore no ground to con-
strue them so, as if the Church, by allowing them, did renounce the ground of all her Christianity. *But not ground
enough to satisfy a reasonable man, that all that make
them do hold that infinite distance between God and His
Saints and Angels, of whom they demand the same effects,
which if they hold not, they are idolaters as the Heathen
were:* who being convinced of one Godhead, as the
Fathers challenge to their faces, divided it into one prin-

cipal, and divers that by His gift are such. *How shall I presume, that simple Christians, in the devotions of their hearts, understand that distance of God from His creatures which their words signify not? which the wisest of their teachers will be much troubled to say, by what figure of speech they can allow it?* Especially if it be considered how little reason or interest in religion there can be to advance this reverence of Christian people towards the Saints or Angels so far above the reason and ground, which ought to be the spring-head of it. For so far are we from any tradition of the Catholic Church for this, that the admonition of Epiphanius to the Collyridians takes hold of it.—So doth the admonition of S. Ambrose* (in Rom. i.) to them who reserve nothing to God, that they give not to His servants. So doth that of S. Augustine, (de Vera Rel. cap. lv.) that our religion is not to consist in worshipping the dead; and that an Angel forbad S. John to worship him, but only God; Whose fellow-servants they were. So doth the argument of S. Gregory Nyssene, (contra Eunom. iv.) and Athanasius, (contra Arian. iii.) concluding our Lord to be God, because He is worshipped, which Cornelius was forbid by S. Peter, S. John by the the Angel, to do to them, saith Athanasius.

" In fine, so dangerous is the case, that whoso communicateth in it, is no way reasonably assured that he communicateth not in the worship of Idols. Only the Church of England having acknowledged the Church of Rome a true Church, though corrupt, ever since the Reformation, I am obliged so to interpret the prayers thereof, as to acknowledge the corruption so great, that the prayers which it alloweth, may be idolatries, if they be made in that sense which they may properly signify: but not that they are necessarily idolatries. For if they were necessarily idolatries, then were the Church of Rome necessarily no Church; the being of Christianity presupposing the wor-

* Ambrosiaster.

I

ship of One true God. And though, to confute the
Heretics, the style of modern devotions leaves nothing
to God, which is not attributed to and desired of His
Saints ; yet it cannot be denied they may be the words of
them who believe that God alone can give that which they
desire.

" The second sort, it is confessed, had the beginning in
the flourishing times of the Church after Constantine ᵐ.
The lights of the Greek and Latin Church, Basil, Nazianzen, Nyssen, Ambrose, Jerome, Augustine, Chrysostom,
Cyrils both, Theodoret, Fulgentius, Gregory the Great,
Leo, more or rather all after that time, have all of them
spoken to the Saints departed, and desired their assistance.
But neither is this enough to make a tradition of the
Church. For the Church had been three hundred years
before it began. Irenæus is mistaken, when he is
alleged for it, as I said even now. Card. Bellarmine
alleges out of Eusebius de Preparat. xiii. 10. ' We
make our prayers to them.' But the Greek bears only,
' We make our prayers to God at their monuments.'
Athanasius de Sanctissima Deipara, whom he quotes, is
certainly of a later date than Athanasiusⁿ. Out of S.

ᵐ Dr. Butler, (Lect. 12. p. 307.) alleging this passage, omits
Thorndike's statement that this practice began in the times of
Constantine, and quotes the rest thus, " It is confessed, adds the
learned and impartial Thorndike, that *all* the Fathers both of the
Greek and Latin Churches, &c." to " assistance."

ⁿ Still quoted by Dr. Wiseman thus, " S. Athanasius, the
most zealous and strenuous supporter, that the Church ever
possessed, of the Divinity of Jesus Christ, and consequently of His
infinite superiority over all the saints, thus enthusiastically
addresses His ever-blessed Mother," (Lect. 13. p. 108.) yet the
very edition from which he professes to quote, the Benedictine,
pronounces the work spurious. It is quoted also by Dr. Butler,
Lect. 3. " The singular devotion of the Catholic Church to the
Blessed Virgin Mary justified." p. 103. On the same subject

Hilary I see nothing brought nor remember any thing to be brought to that purpose. In fine, after Constantine, when the Festivals of the Saints, being publicly celebrated, occasioned the confluence of Gentiles as well as Christians, and innumerable things were done, which seemed miracles done by God, to attest the honour done them, and the truth of Christianity which it supposed, I acknowledge those great lights did think fit to address themselves to them as petitioners ; but so at the first, as those that were no ways assured by our common Christianity, that their petitions arrived at their knowledge. You have seen S. Augustine acknowledge that they must come by such means, as God is no way tied to furnish. Greg. Nazianz. speaks to Gorgonia in his oration upon her, and to Constantius, in his first oration against Julian, but under a doubtful condition, if they were sensible of what he spake. Enough to distinguish praying to God, from any address to a creature, though religion be the ground of it. And

Mr. Phillips in a solitary quotation from the Fathers, alleges in justification of the shocking Psalter, called St. Bonaventure's, "the great S. Augustine;" yet the Benedictines again call the homily, (which is given to S. Augustine in the Breviary,) "the work of some unskilful patchwork-maker." (on Serm. 194. App. al. de Sanctis 18.) Again, Dr. Wiseman in his recent Letter to Mr. Palmer, quotes confidently on the same subject, as words of S. Ephraem, certain prayers found mostly in a solitary *Greek* MS. of which Cave (Hist. Lit. s. tit.) says, "Beyond question not Ephraem's ; sequiorum sæculorum deliramentum," and as S. Gregory of Nazianzum's, some from the Christus Patiens, which both the Benedictines and the recent editor pronounce not to be his, and the Benedictines say of the words, that "they savour at least of the age of Damascene, or even one much later than the 8th or 9th." Romanist citations of the fathers always require to be sifted ; their system not being really founded on Antiquity, but on the authority of the existing Church, they are careless how they quote.

when the apparitions about their monuments were held unquestionable, yet it was questioned, whether the same soul would be present at once in places of so much distance, or Angels appear like them, as you may see in the answer aforesaid, p. 391. 394. Nay, Hugo de S. Victore in Cassander, Epist. xix. hath enabled him to hold, that the Litanies do not suppose that the Saints hear them, and therefore are expounded by some to signify conditional desires, if God grant them to come to their knowledge. But of that I speak not yet, only as it enables me, to conclude, that this kind of prayer is not idolatry. This necessarily follows from the premises; because a man cannot take that Saint or Angel for God, whose prayers he desires;—but manifestly shews that his desire is grounded upon the relation which he thinks he hath to him, by our Lord Jesus Christ and by His Church. Nevertheless, though it be not idolatry, the consequence and production of it not being distinguishable from idolatry, the Church must needs stand obliged to give it those bounds that may prevent such mischief as that which shall make it no Church."—

It were well if the Romish Church, which so gladly pleads in her behalf the charitable allowances made by Thorndike, that he need not necessarily pronounce her idolatrous, although she tolerates what leads to idolatry, would also consider his warning against her sanctioning practices, which naturally lead to it, and his strong conviction that the existence of such practices, unforbidden by authority, must be "one of the most considerable titles," as for our original "reformation without consent of the whole," so also for continued separation. It is sad to see a serious person[o] thus defend the Invocation, " deliver us, holy Virgin Mary ;"

" Why do not such persons compile a ' dictionary' or a ' speaker's assistant;' in which we may find words to express fully and adequately our thoughts, and the different tempers and motives of our minds?"

Such language, and that cited by Archbishop Ussher, is not only liable to be taken in an unsound sense, but the unsound is its obvious meaning.

Thorndike then thus proceeds ;

" Suppose a simple soul can distinguish between Ora pro nobis, and Domine miserere ; between ' Pray for us,' and ' Lord have mercy upon us ;' how shall I be assured, that it distinguishes between the honour that Pagans gave the less gods, under Jupiter the Father of Gods, and that which himself gives the Saints, under the God of those Saints? And is it enough, that the Church enjoins not nor teaches idolatry? Is it not further bound to secure us against it? I know not whether it can be said that Processions and Litanies are voluntary devotions, which the people are not answerable for, if they neglect. They were first brought in, and since frequented at the instance of Prelates, and their Clergy ; and if they be amiss, the people are snared by their means : that is, by the Church, if the Church bear them out in it. And by these three sorts of Prayers, it appears that without giving bounds to private conceits, there is [no] means to stop men's course from that extremity, which whether it be real idolatry or not, nothing can assure us. Upon these terms I stand. I have heard those relations, upon credit not to be ques-

[o] Dr. Butler, Lect. 12. p. 360.

tioned, which make their devotions to Saints hardly distinguishable from the idolatries of Pagans. That they who preferred them could not, or did not, distinguish, I say not. In fine, they demonstrate manifold more affection for the Blessed Virgin, or some particular Saints, than for our Lord. That they call not upon Saints to pray for them, but to help them ; that they neither express nor can be presumed to mean by praying for, but by granting their prayers; in fine, *that they demonstrate inward subjection of the heart wherein idolatry consists ;* I cannot disbelieve those who relate what they see done. What may be the reason, why to them rather than to God ?"

" I grant it no Idolatry, that is, not *necessarily* any Idolatry, to pray to Saints to pray for us. The very matter implies an equivocation in the word ' praying,' which nothing hinders the heart to distinguish. But is it fit for the Church to maintain it, because it is necessarily no Idolatry ? I grant, ' Ora pro nobis' in the Litanies might be taken for the ejaculation of a desire, which a man knows not whether it is heard or not ; (as some instance in a letter, which a man would write, though uncertain whether it shall come to hand or not ;) and I could wish that the people were taught so much by the form, as a powerful means to preserve the distance between God and His creature alive in their esteem. I count it not fit for a private person to say, what might be condescended to, for the re-union of the Church, stopping the way upon those mischiefs, which the flourishing times of the Church have not prevented. While all bounds are refused, all extremities maintained, I allege it for one of the most considerable titles for reformation without the consent of the whole."

Enough will now have been said to vindicate the distinction between the occasional addresses, which occur in the fourth century, requesting the prayers of the Saints, and the systematic devotions prevalent in the Romish Church, requesting their aid absolutely, and preferring them, upon system, to immediate application to our Lord. Since this distinction is so broad, and appeared so to such writers as Archbishops Ussher and Bramhall [a], Bp. Andrews [b], and Thorndike, there is clearly no ground, why we should suppose that our Article, in condemning the " Romish doctrine of Invocation of Saints," had any reference to these addresses of the fourth century. At the same time, persons cannot be too strongly warned against the risk to their own souls, in resuming, even in its lightest form, a practice, which does not come recommended to us by the Primitive Church, and which Scripture, to say the least, in principle, discourages; which, as a *systematic* practice, does not seem to be countenanced even by the age in which it was introduced, the addresses in the fourth century being rather apostrophes to the blessed Saints who were at the moment before the minds of those who used them, than systematic requests for their intercession. And yet even this alone would obviously make a great difference in the religious influence of such addresses; the *systematic* application for their intercessions has

[a] Works, p. 418, quoted in Mr. Newman's Letter to Dr. Jelf, p. 14.
[b] Answer to c. 20. of Card. Perron's Reply, p. 57—62. quoted Tract 90, p. 41, 2.

manifestly a tendency, which such occasional apostrophes as we find in the fourth century at all
events have not, to give them a place in our
thoughts which should be occupied only by the One
Intercessor. Systematic addresses to them constitute them, so far, direct objects of our devotions, which having, as our friend observes, " less
of awe and severity," may be gradually resorted
to in preference, in order to " save men the
necessity of lifting up their minds to their Sanctifier and their Judge." It is to be considered,
whether *habitual* addresses to the Saints do not,
in the mildest form, imply that they are *themselves*,
in some degree, objects of devotion. In the case of
friends on earth, with which these addresses are
paralleled, we are content to ask their intercessions once for all, or as an emergency occurs;
we do not habitually ask them to " pray for us;"
we take it for granted that they do; the continual
use then of these supplications to the Saints, (who,
as being purified, must love us better, and be more
ready to pray for us than our friends on earth,)
seems in itself to imply that some other feeling
has crept in, beyond the wish to secure their
intercessions; that people apply to them, as a
vent to their feelings; that they have uncon-
sciously made them ends and objects of devotion,
and are thereby associating other objects in their
devotional feelings with their One lawful Object,
our Maker, Redeemer, Sanctifier; are learning to

have recourse to them, together with Him and in His place. There is also in itself so much risk in addressing prayers to one unseen, who is not God; it is, on the one hand, so much an act of devotion, and on the other, our devotions to God are at best so imperfect, so little elevated, that there is on this ground alone much risk, lest the acts of devotion to the creature and to the Creator should be of the same kind, and so those to the creature idolatrous. The very fact that we find these appeals first in very holy men, may be (as our friend observes) a ground to discourage such as we are, not to encourage us; the less like them we are, the less should we imitate them in this one point. " It [c] is nothing to the purpose to urge the example of such men as S. Bernard, in defence of such invocations. The holier the man, the less likely they are to be injurious to him; but it is another matter entirely when ordinary persons do the same." There would be also an especial risk in such practices in our own Church, beyond what there is even in the Romish; they do not come recommended to *us* by our immediate Mother, any more than by the Church Catholic; one who should adopt them, would do so on doubtful precedents, and on his own " private judgment;" he would do it altogether on his own responsibility, as his own act, contrary to what his Church deems advisable for

[c] Mr. Newman's Letter to the Bishop of Oxford, p. 19. The whole page is a very valuable warning.

her children generally, and as I said, having no sanction (as in the case of prayers for the Saints at rest) from the Church Catholic; he ought also to have fears lest he be actuated herein by mixed motives, such as imagination, excitement, novelty, and so to doubt the lawfulness of the action in himself, over and above its abstract questionableness : he can, or ought, hardly to feel absolutely assured of its propriety, and ought then well to consider, why he does not come under the Apostle's rule, " He that doubteth is damned if he eat, for whatsoever is not of faith is sin."   Lastly, if any ever so much desire to have the intercession of those, who see their Redeemer face to face, it is so safe to ask Him to put in their minds to pray Him for them, so unsafe to apply to them directly, that they must, surely, feel that they are exposing themselves very gratuitously to risk in adopting a practice to which there are so many grave objections, when the object they have at heart can be obtained more surely, because sought for more humbly, without it.

I need only, in conclusion, express the earnest hope, in which you will so strongly join, that any one, who after the example of our friend, finds himself called upon to give an opinion that " the *ora pro nobis* is not necessarily included in the Invocation of Saints, which the Article condemns," will follow him also in expressing his " great apprehension concerning the use even of such modified invocations[d]." And altogether, the less such a subject is discussed, obviously the better; the very mention of it may prove a snare to some minds, who are not trained in those feelings of reverence, which happily prevail in this place; it is not and ought not to be a practical question to us; but the abstract discussion of questions involving great practical consequences, yet unfelt by those discussing them, is too likely to divest the mind of those feelings of solemn responsibility without which no religious question can be discussed without injury.

4, 5. *Veneration and worshipping of Images and Relics.*

The less need be said on this, the remaining subject of this Article, because, although the feeling of the Ancient Church with regard to relics was very different from that common now, there was no view in any part of it which any way approximated to the Romish doctrine or practice. On the contrary, the primitive doctrine and prac-

---

[d] Meanwhile, it is very comforting to see younger men also alive to this especial danger, "Through the course which Mr. N. has now been obliged to take, the ' ora pro nobis' may have been brought before persons, who would otherwise never have thought of it, and who may take it up from the mere affectation of singularity or what may be called a restless love of newly seen and dimly apprehended truth." A Few More Words in Support of No. 90, &c. by Rev. W. G. Ward.

tice, on the subject of images, was so strict, that the difficulty would rather be to reconcile the " having" images at all, with it ; of worship or outward reverence there was no trace. I will not here repeat what I hope shortly to give at length ; I will only then mention to you the result of a careful examination, in which I sifted every thing alleged about images in the early centuries. This I have thus summed up [e];

" 1. In the three first centuries it is positively stated that the Christians had no images. 2. Private individuals had pictures, but it was discouraged. (Aug.) 3. The Cross, not the Crucifix, was used ; the first mention of the Cross in a Church is in the time of Constantine. 4. The first mention of pictures in Churches (except to forbid them) is at the end of the fourth century ; and these, historical pictures from the O. T. or of martyrdoms, not of individuals. 5. No account of any picture of our Lord being publicly used occurs in the six first centuries, (the first is in Leontius Neap. l. v. Apol. pro Christian. A. D. 600.) 6. Outward reverence to pictures is condemned." '[And this as late as Gregory M., who speaks in his genuine works very decisively against outward reverence to images, the passage apologizing for it being spurious.]

One cannot again imagine any thing more strikingly opposed to the Romish apologies for their worship before images, or a more valuable warning against their peril, than the following passage of S. Augustine [f];

    [e] Library of the Fathers ; Tertullian.   Note B. on Apology, p. 116.
    [f] In Ps. 113. Serm. 2. §. 5.

" Who worships or prays, *looking upon an image*, and does not become so affected as to think that he is heard by it, as to hope that what he longs for will be granted him by it ?—Against this feeling, whereby human and carnal infirmity may easily be ensnared, the Scripture of God utters things well known, whereby it reminds and rouses as it were the minds of men, slumbering in the accustomed things of the body ; ' The images of the heathen,' it says, ' are silver and gold.' " He then (§. 6.) meets the objection, that the Christians too had *vessels* of silver and gold, the works of men's hands, for the service of the Sacraments. " But," he asks, " have they mouths, and speak not ? have they eyes, and see not ? do we pray to them, in that, through them, we pray to God ? This is the chief cause of that frantic ungodliness, that a form, like one living, has more power over the feelings of the unhappy beings, causing itself to be worshipped, than the plain fact that it is not living, so that it ought to be despised by the living. For images are of more avail to bow down the unhappy mind (in that they have mouth, have eyes, have ears, have nostrils, have hands, have feet,) than it hath to correct it that they speak not, see not, hear not, smell not, touch not, walk not."

With regard to " relics" on the other hand, the later corruptions have given a turn to our *feelings*, at variance with those of the early Church, though their practice did not differ from our's. The Roman practice condemned, appears, from the Homilies, to have been the " offering incense [h]" to the reliques ; and of this or of any other outward veneration to them, no traces are pretended to be

---

[h] Homily on Good Works, P. 2. p. 54. On Peril of Idolatry, P. 3. p. 220, 249.

found in the Ancient Church.   Those who love the
early Church have to regret a tone of mind, which
seems estranged from her's ; yet was there nothing
in her practice which modern notions could include
under the censure of " veneration of relics."   There
is no question then as to the interpretation of the
Article ; only as to the tone of mind of those who
expound them, lest they speak slightingly of sacred
feelings, and, as I said, foster the principle of
rejecting the evidence of miracles, like the Jews or
modern Deists, on à priori grounds.   The feeling
about   relics,   too   common   among   us,   is   sadly
natural.   Who would not of himself love, as they of
old did, the ashes of the " noble army of martyrs ?"
or whose eyes would not gush out with tears at
sight of a fragment of the true Cross ? who would
not (in St. Jerome's[i] words) " worship prostrate
before it, as though he saw the Lord hanging
thereon ?" who can even realize to himself the
awful reality of what he should feel ? and yet, in
proportion as he would love them, if he had
ground to believe them real, he must grieve over
the avarice of men, which so multiplied them, that
our later Church knows not where she has them.
Nor is it strange that the lying miracles of later
days, connected with supposed relics, should create
a repugnance to believe true miracles, wrought by
God in connection with the true.   Yet to persist,
against evidence, to deny earlier miracles, were to act

[i] In vit. Paulæ Ep. 108. §. 9.

upon passion, not on the love of the truth. Rather, since God did work miracles by them in those days, one should, on that ground, adhere the more closely to that Faith, which He attested by miracles, and the more look with reverence and longing to those holy days, when God vouchsafed to form saints whom He crowned with martyrdom, and copy the practices whereby they were so formed, and seek by a holy life the indwelling of that Holy Spirit, which so hallowed even the " dry bones" of those who had been so eminently His temple, that they still " lived," and " being dead, yet spake," and became to others the source of earthly, and thereby also of spiritual, life and healing.

The several instances of the respect paid by the Ancient Church to " relics" are embodied in the following vindication by Thorndike[1]; in which no one of our Church, (whatever vague impressions he may have had,) will probably find any thing which he would wish to gainsay.

" He that could wish, that the memories of the Martyrs, and other Saints who lived so as to assure the Church they would have been Martyrs had they been called to it, had not been honoured, as it is plain they were honoured by Christians, must find in his heart by consequence to wish that Christianity had not prevailed. For, this honour, depending on nothing but assurance of their happiness, in them that remained alive, was that which moved unbelievers to bethink themselves of the

i Epilogue iii. 30. p. 354.

reason they had to be Christians.   What were then those honours?   Reverence in preserving the remains of their bodies and burying them, celebrating the remembrance of their agonies every year, assembling themselves at their monuments, making the days of their death festivals, the place of burial Churches, building and consecrating Churches to the service of God in remembrance of them, I will add further, (for the custom seemeth to come from undefiled Christianity,) burying the remains of their bodies under the stones upon which the Eucharist was celebrated.   What was there in all this but Christianity? That the circumstances of God's service, which no law of God had limited, the time, the place, the occasion of assembling for the service of God (always acceptable to God) should be determined by such glorious accidents for Christianity, as the departure of those, who had thus concluded their race.   What can be so properly counted the reign of the Saints and Martyrs with Christ, which St. John foretelleth, Apoc. xx. as this honour, when it came to trample Paganism under feet, after the conversion of Constantine?   Certainly, nothing can be named, so correspondent to that honour which is prophesied for them that suffered for God's law, under Antiochus Epiphanes. Dan. xii.   Is not all this honour properly derivative from the honour of God and our Lord Jesus Christ, and relative to His service?   For, that is the work for which Christians assemble, and for those assemblies the Church stands, as I have often said; the honour of the Saints, but the occasion, circumstance, or furniture for it."

Art. xxxii.

" Bishops, Priests, and Deacons, are not commanded by God's law, either to vow the estate of single life, or to abstain from marriage."

" There is," as our friend said, " no subject for controversy in these words, since even the most determined advocates of the celibacy of the clergy admit their truth." Not only S. Jerome, whom he quotes, but even modern Romanists rest clerical celibacy on ecclesiastical rule, not on " God's law." On the other hand, it should be observed, that the tone of the Article is contrary to men's modern practice; it does not take it for granted, as a matter of course, that clergymen will marry, as soon as they can provide for a family ; as if this were obviously the best both for themselves and those committed to them ; but it implies, as does the Marriage Service for all, that it is a matter of Christian prudence and wisdom to decide, in which estate, married or single, they may best serve the Lord, and that they will decide, not with a view to earthly joy, but " as they shall judge the same to serve better to godliness."

A contemporary document implies the feeling of those times to have been in favour of the celibacy of the Clergy ; our Marriage Service goes further, and, in the midst of its touching commendation of the " honourable estate" of matrimony, implies a holy celibacy to be for those to

K

whom it is given, a higher state. For in that it speaks of " continency" as a " gift," it must imply that it is an especial favour of God to those to whom it is given.

> " Although[a] it were not only better for the estimation of Priests, and other Ministers in the Church of God, to live chaste, sole, and separate from the company of women and the bond of marriage, but also thereby they might the better attend to the administration of the Gospel, and be less intricated and troubled with the charge of household, being free and unburdened from the care and cost of finding wife and children, and that it were most to be wished, that they would willingly and of themselves endeavour themselves to a perpetual chastity and abstinence from the use of women."

In the Lord's vineyard, however, there is ample room for those of both classes ; our Universities still furnish an instance before our eyes, of institutions requiring a temporary celibate, and that during the most trying period of life, and often for the greater part of its probable term : and, as this shews that it is not foreign to the genius of our Church, so the conviction is continually growing, that if the degraded masses condensed in our overgrown towns, inaccessible to any means now existing, festering within themselves, yet shunning every thing unlike themselves, may yet be reclaimed, it will be, when God raises up among us men of self-denying habits, who, under the direction of our Bishops, shall gather round them others like-minded, and form

[a] Stat. An. 2 and 3 Edw. VI. c. 21.

corresponding institutions for those who have " forsaken all" to " follow" their Lord, to seek out His
scattered sheep even in these appalling wildernesses,
and preach repentance from dead works, Judgment
to come, and the vanity of this fleeting world, having
themselves, like the self-denying Baptist, visibly no
portion in it.

It is, again, felt continually more, that besides
the domestic charities so lovelily set forth by the
daughters of our land, there is room for institutions,
in which such as have no sacred duties at home, may
devote their whole lives to visit their Lord in His
sick, poor, imprisoned, naked, hungry, thirsty members[n]. Such institutions do shed a lustre upon any

[n] Since the above was written, the following remarkable confirmation has occurred in a Preface written to controvert what the
Author supposes to be the peculiar views of Mr. Newman and his
friends.   Amid grave difference of opinion, the tone of the whole
Preface seems to betoken a drawing together of men's minds,
even when they must still oppose each other, and deprecate any
extension of that which is peculiar to the other.   The whole
passage is very illustrative of what Mr. Newman has said of the
moving " of the religious mind of our Church to something better
and truer than satisfied the last century."

" No wise man doubts that the Reformation was imperfect, or
that in the Romish system there were many good institutions,
and practices, and feelings, which it would be most desirable to
restore amongst ourselves.   Daily church services, frequent communions, memorials of our Christian calling continually presented
to our notice, in crosses and way-side oratories; commemorations
of holy men, of all times and countries, the doctrine of the communion of saints practically taught, religious orders, especially of
women, of different kinds, and under different rules, delivered
only from the snare and sin of perpetual vows; all these, most of

Church; they are evidences of self-denying holiness fostered within it; the "sœurs de la charite" not only create a rightful sympathy towards the Churches wherein they exist, but they are one of the most powerful attractions to withdraw feeling but undisciplined minds from the communion of our own; they would be a grace to us, if we had them; the lack of them exposes us to loss. On this account alone, then, people should beware how they lightly speak against the celibate as a whole. Yet probably the objection arises from confusing *compulsory* with voluntary celibacy; the high feelings of devotedness which would with joy realize such a calling do exist among us; and it need, I think, but be known that there are (as there are) means provided for exercising such a calling under protection, and we too shall have our "sisters of charity." Parents willingly part with a daughter for an earthly bridal; some will be

which are of some efficacy for good, even in a corrupt church, belong no less to the true Church, and would be purely beneficial." (Preface to Dr. Arnold's Sermons on the Christian Life, p. lvi. v.)

There is no need of "perpetual vows;" in France vows are allowed by the State to be taken only for five years; any vow should, of course, be taken with much humility and circumspection, and after trial and acquired knowledge of a person's own strength and weakness; only it does not appear why, when "perpetual vows" are permitted and encouraged in the Old Testament, and that even by parents in behalf of their children, (as in the case of Samuel, not to speak of Samson,) they should, under the New, in which greater strength is given, be accounted as necessarily "a sin."

found to spare them to be " brides of Christ," ministers to Him in His sick.

On the other hand, *our* Reformation stands clear from that sad and inexplicable act of foreign Reformers, (which Romanists so willingly impute to all[o],) when they deliberately sanctioned a Prince's polygamy[p] as a remedy against a grosser adultery: our Reformers were bound by no vows to celibacy[q], so that Cranmer who married, broke none ; others voluntarily abstained from that, which they wished to be left free to each, as they should " judge the same to serve better to godliness," thereby shewing that they advocated its legality, not as a skreen for themselves, but as thinking *compulsory* celibacy inexpedient and dangerous.   In our Church no nun[r] was tempted to break her vows.

On this whole subject, it were well if before people allow themselves to use or to listen to the hard speeches which have of late years been uttered against the notion of celibacy as a religious act, or the view of it in the Ancient Church, they would consider how they escape therein speaking against their Lord.   Certainly, the principle of religious celi-

---

[o] e. g. Dr. Butler, Lect. 5. p. 250. 267.

[p] The dispensation given by Luther, Melancthon, Bucer, and four others, to the Landgrave of Hesse, to marry a second wife, in the lifetime of the first.

[q] " The vow of chastity, which existed in the Ordination-service of the foreign Churches, formed no part of that used in England." Short, Hist. of Eng. Ch. §. 311.

[r] Dr. Butler, l. c. p. 267.   Exactly the same things were brought forward before him by Dr. Milner, End of Controversy.

bacy is so plainly set down by Himself, that it seems to imply a strange ignorance or sad neglect of His word, to dare to call that principle in question. And His word is not like S. Paul's limited, by "the present distress [a]," but, like Himself, eternal. Our Church, as I said, recognises that principle in her Marriage Service. I will now but set down those His words, and, with Thorndike's [b] comment on them, so leave the subject.

" Matt. xix. 11, 12. All are not capable of this word (of not marrying). 'For there are eunuchs which were so born from their mother's womb ; and there are eunuchs which were made eunuchs by men : and there are eunuchs that have made themselves eunuchs for the kingdom of Heaven. He that is capable let him hold this.' Here it is said that God hath made some men of such constitution of nature, that they are able to contain themselves from marriage, and that this is the gift of continence, which whoso hath, falls under a command of not marrying ; whoso hath not, of marrying. But when our Lord exhorts those that are able to contain themselves from marriage to strive for that grace, certainly He makes not that a gift of nature, which He would have a man endeavour to attain. He that is exhorted to make himself an eunuch is not so made by God, but from God he hath the grace to prefer the kingdom of Heaven before even that content which God alloweth him here ; and if he betray not that grace, by preferring that content before the clearest and securest means of attaining it, he will not fail of grace to perform that which he resolves for God's sake. And truly it were strange that the Gospel should make that grace which

[a] 1 Cor. vii.

[b] Epilogue, p. ii. c. 33. p. 296.

conducts to the height of Christianity, to consist in an endowment of nature."

Article xxxvii.

" The Bishop of Rome hath no jurisdiction in this realm of England."

I only set this Article down, that I may not seem to omit any thing, yet there is no question to be raised upon it. It relates to temporals, not to spirituals. The " jurisdiction of the Bishop of Rome" stands contrasted with " the chief power of the King's Majesty," and this is, in the Article itself, limited to things temporal. The Article is entitled, " Of the Civil Magistrates." It begins by claiming the " chief power or government of all estates of this realm, whether they be Ecclesiastical or Civil, in all causes" to the " King's Majesty," and denies that it " ought to be subject to any foreign jurisdiction." It then explains the " chief Government" claimed for the King, negatively, not to be " the ministering either of God's word or of the Sacraments," and positively to be only, " that they should rule all estates and degrees committed to their charge by God, whether they be ecclesiastical or temporal, and restrain with the civil sword the stubborn and evil-doers." Accordingly, its chief object is to deny the right of appeal to Rome in the case of ecclesiastical persons or causes. Then it subjoins the words prefixed above. Clearly, then, from the whole tenor of the Article, the "jurisdiction" denied is a "temporal jurisdiction as to spiritual causes or persons." And this is illustrated by the oath of supremacy. "No foreign prince, person, prelate, state, or potentate, hath or ought to have any jurisdiction, power, superiority, preeminence, or authority within this realm." Both deny to the Bishop of Rome, what and what only they claim to the King. The oath of supremacy is a negative oath of allegiance. It rejects all allegiance which may interfere with the allegiance to the King. The very terms of the oath of supremacy, (in that it puts together "prelate, state, potentate,") imply that what it contemplates is any such "jurisdiction," as shall interfere with the authority of the sovereign. Thus Archbishop Bramhall [r];

"Whatsoever power our Laws did divest the Pope of, they invested the King with it: but they never invested the King with any Spiritual power or jurisdiction; witness the Injunctions of Queen Elizabeth; witness the public Articles of the Church; witness the professions of King James; witness all our Statutes themselves, wherein all the parts of Papal power are enumerated which are taken away; his Encroachments, his Usurpations, his Oaths, his Collations, Provisions, Pensions, Tenths, First-fruits, Reservations, Palls, Unions Commendam, Exemptions, Dispensations of all kinds, Confirmations, Licenses, Faculties, Suspensions, Appeals, and God knoweth how many pecuniary artifices more: but of them all, there is not

[r] Schism guarded, sect. i. c. 9. Works, p. 340. referred to in Palmer on the Church, p. ii. c. 2.

one that concerneth Jurisdiction purely Spiritual, or which is an Essential right of the power of the Keys; they are all Branches of the External Regiment of the Church, the greater part of them usurped from the Crown, sundry of them from the Bishops, and some found out by the Popes themselves, as the payment for Palls, which was nothing in St. Gregory's time, but a free gift or liberality or bounty, free from imposition and exaction.

" Lastly, consider the grounds of all our grievances expressed frequently in our Laws, and in other writers, the disinheriting of the Prince and Peers, the destruction and annullation of the Laws and the prerogative Royal, the vexation of the King's Liege People, the impoverishing of the Subjects, the draining the Kingdom of its Treasure, the decay of Hospitality, the disservice of God, and filling the Churches of England with Foreigners, the excluding Temporal Kings and Princes out of their Dominions, the Subjecting of the Realm to spoil and ravine, gross Simoniacal Contracts, Sacrilege, grievous and intolerable oppressions and extortions. Jurisdiction purely Spiritual doth neither disinherit the Prince nor the Peers, nor destroy and annul the Laws and Prerogative Royal, nor vex the King's Liege People, nor impoverish the Subject, nor drain the Kingdom of its Treasures, nor fill the Churches with Foreigners, nor exclude Temporal Kings out of their Dominions, nor subject the Realm to spoil and ravine. Authority purely Spiritual is not guilty of the Decay of Hospitality or disservice of Almighty God, or Simony, or Sacrilege, or oppressions and extortions. No, no, it is the external Regiment of the Church, by new Roman Laws and Mandates, by new Roman Sentences and Judgments, by new Roman Pardons and Dispensations, by new Roman Synods and Oaths of Fidelity, by new Roman Bishops and Clerks. It is your new Roman Tenths and First-fruits and Provisions and Reservations and Pardons and Indulgences, and the rest of those horrible mischiefs and damnable customs, that are apparently guilty of all these evils. These Papal Innovations we have taken away indeed, and deservedly, having shewed the express time, and place, and person, when and where, and by whom every one of them was first introduced into England.

And again[x],

" We have only cast out seven or eight branches of Papal jurisdiction in the exterior court ; which Christ or His Apostles never challenged, never exercised, never meddled with ; which the Church never granted, never disposed. He might still for us enjoy his Protopatriarchate, and the dignity of an Apostolical Bishop, and his primacy of order, so long as the Church thought fit to continue it to that See, if this would content him."

Or again, to take the words of a recent author, following Abp. Bramhall[y].

" The learned primate Bramhall has observed, that these acts were not intended to deprive the Roman Pontiff of any really spiritual power ; they only cast out some branches of his exterior jurisdiction which were not instituted by Christ, nor by the Catholic Church. They did not deny the precedency of the Bishop of Rome in the Universal Church, nor his right (in conjunction with Christian princes) of summoning and presiding in General Councils, nor his power of defining questions of faith in conjunction with the Catholic Church, nor his right to exhort all Bishops to observe the Canons, nor his being the centre of Catholic unity, when he is in communion with all the Catholic Church. None of these things (the chief privileges of the Roman primacy according to Romanists)

[x] ib. sect. 5.
[y] Palmer, l. c.

were affected by the Acts of Parliament for abolishing the usurped jurisdiction of the Roman Bishop in England; and therefore it is vain to impute schism or heresy to the Church of England on this account, even on the supposition that the primacy of the Roman See is of divine institution."

I do not mean, of course, to imply by this, that the Bishop of Rome has any lawful claims to " spiritual supremacy" over us ; our very acknowledgment of our Articles implies our sense of a right committed to us, to regulate the affairs of our Church (whenever this should be necessary) by and for ourselves. I only mean, as a matter of fact, that any discussions as to any spiritual authority of the Bishop of Rome,—supposing that he was in communion with the whole Church, or that he would acknowledge its authority to be superior to his own,—is foreign to this Article, which relates to things temporal only. Meanwhile, it may be said that a primacy of order, and the claim that no Council should be considered Œcumenical and authoritative which lacked the concurrence of so eminent a See, as they will abundantly satisfy both the concessions of any of the early fathers, and the claims of the earlier Popes, so may they be obviously conceded without any risk to the safety of our Provincial Church.

On the same ground, lest I should appear to gloss over any thing, I would just advert to three other

Articles not relating to questions in which we are at issue with the Romish system, and apparently not contemplated by those, who condemned the principles of the Tract. So much has been written on them lately, that I may be the more brief here.

Article xi.

" That we are justified by Faith only, is a most wholesome doctrine."

On Article xi. our friend contends, that " Justification by faith only," as the instrument through which we receive it, does not exclude " Baptism" from being the instrument through which God conveys it ; and this is indeed so palpable from the Article itself, which is contrasting only " the merits of our Lord and Saviour Jesus Christ," received " through faith," with " our own works or deservings," that it seems strange how any should have thought that the doctrine of Baptism entered at all into the subject of this Article. The Article simply contrasts " the merits of our Lord and Saviour" and " our works," and says we are justified for the sake of the one, not of the other ; it is employed in laying down one principle, not in stating the whole compass of divinity ; the doctrine of the Sacraments comes in elsewhere ; the Article contrasts, as the source or meritorious

causes of Justification, " the Merits of our Lord"
and " our own merits ;" and these would naturally
exclude each other; but " our Lord's merit" as the
" sole *source* of our justification" does not exclude
" Baptism" as the " sole channel" through which
He conveys it, any more than it does faith as the
sole instrument through which we receive it. The
whole is concisely worded thus [a];

" We are justified by Christ alone, in that He has purchased the gift ; by Faith alone, in that Faith asks for it;
by Baptism alone, for Baptism conveys it ; and by
newness of heart alone, for newness of heart is the life
of it."

Articles xii. and xiii.

" Works done before the grace of Christ and the
inspiration of His Spirit [' before justification,' title of the
Article] are not pleasant to God (minimè Deo grata sunt)
forasmuch as they spring not of Faith in Jesus Christ,
neither do they make man meet to receive grace, or (as the
School authors say) deserve grace of congruity (merentur
gratiam de congruo); yea, rather for that they are not
done as God hath willed and commanded them to be done,
we doubt not but they have the nature of sin. Albeit
good works, which are the fruits of faith and follow after
justification (justificatos sequuntur), cannot put away
(expiare) our sins and endure the severity of God's judgment, yet are they pleasing and acceptable (grata et ac-
cepta) to God in Christ, and do spring out necessarily of a
true and lively faith."

As, in Article xi. " the merits of our Lord" are

[a] Tract 90, p. 13.

contrasted with " our own," so in Articles xii. and
xiii. our own works before and after justification
are broadly contrasted with each other ; and one
chief object of the two Articles plainly is, to carry
out the contrast of Article xi., and to declare that
our works are no ways the meritorious cause of our
acceptableness with God;—not those before justification, because " they are not done as God hath
willed and commanded them to be done," and so
" have the nature of sin ;" nor those after, because
1) they " cannot put away our sins," nor 2) even
in themselves " endure the severity of God's judgment ;"—and therefore we must on both grounds
have recourse to the merits of our Lord to efface
our sins, and obtain a merciful judgment for our
good works.   We are, then, thus contemplated in
these Articles, as in two conditions, " justified"
and " unjustified," and our works are declared
broadly and on the whole, in our unjustified state
to have " the nature of sin ;" good works, in our
justified state, are said to be " pleasing and acceptable to God in Christ."   But although, to
use our friend's strong words in another place [b], of
our state by nature,

" all that we do, whether from better principles or
from worse, whether of an indifferent nature or directly
moral, whether spontaneously, or habitually, or accident-
ally, all is pervaded with a quality of evil so odious to

[b] On Justification, p. 97.

Almighty God, as to convert even our best services into profanations ; or, in the expressive words of St. Paul, ' They that are in the flesh cannot please God ;' "

it does not follow, of course, that all works " before justification" have equally " the nature of sin." Each of these states,—justification, or being unjustified,—admits of infinite variations and degrees, from theirs who are all but angels to theirs who are all but devils. As being justified or no, they may be considered as two states ; but the individuals included under them may be in an infinite variety of relations to Almighty God. Taken as two states, the " justified" must include all, from those who have all but attained to perfection, to those in whom " the things which remain" "are ready to die," and themselves are all but out of their justified state : on the other hand, of those not justified, some may be almost Christians, others " past feeling," or without any trace of the life of God in them or of His image. But since there can be no good thing in any one, except through the Spirit of God and the grace of Christ, they who are " almost Christians" can not have become such except through His grace and inspiration ; they are being " drawn by the Father" and so are in some way acceptable to Him, although, in that they are *being* drawn, and not actually " come" to the Son, they are not yet justified : still they and their actions are in an intermediate state ; they are not justified, nor their good actions like the " good works" of the justified ; and yet neither are they nor their actions like those whose heart the Holy Spirit has not moved nor influenced their actions. Cornelius was in a degree " accepted with God ;" his " righteousness, worked" through the Divine aid, his " prayers" and his " alms" had " gone up for a memorial before God ;" still he was not yet justified ; for the angel, who tells him " thy prayer is heard, and thine alms are had in remembrance in the sight of God," bade him also send for St. Peter, " who shall tell thee words, whereby thou and all thy house shall be saved." Again, as Bishop Bull points out, since repentance and faith are required of those who come to be baptized, and repentance is not a simple feeling, but one issuing in various actions, there must be, in all cases, before justification, actions in their degree accepted by God, yet accepted not as man's own, but His, Whose gift repentance and the works of repentance are. To hear Bishop Bull [c] :

" Proceed we to the second class of testimonies, those namely in which some special works are prescribed as altogether necessary to salvation. Hereto belong passages which require repentance, as an antecedent condition, without which no one obtains forgiveness of sins from God. Such occur every where in the New Testament ; to take then one or two only ; Acts ii. 38. ' Repent, and be baptized every one of you in the Name of Jesus Christ for the remission of sins, and ye shall receive the gift of the Holy Ghost ;' and Acts iv. 19. ' Repent therefore,

[c] Harm. Apost. c. 2. §. 6, 7.

and 'be converted, that your sins may be blotted out,
when the times of refreshing shall come from the Presence
of the Lord.'   In these places, any one must see that
besides faith, repentance from sin also, and turning to
God, are required of necessity for the remission of sins or
justification."

" It is further to be observed, that repentance is not
one, or a single work, but the complex, as it were, of
many other works.   For it comprehends within its compass the following works, which are neither few nor of
slight account.   1) Sorrow for sins, (2 Cor. vii. 10.)
2) Humiliation under the hand of God, whereby a person
humbly acknowledges that he deserves the Divine wrath,
(Jas. iv. 10.)   3) Hatred and detestation of sins, (Ezek. vi.
9. xx. 43. xxxvi. 31.)   4) Confession of sins, (1 Joh. i. 9.)
5) Earnest and lowly entreaty of the Divine mercy, (Acts
viii. 2.)   6) The love of God, (Ex. xx. 6.)   7) Ceasing
from sin, (Prov. xxviii. 13. Is. i. 16.)   8) A firm purpose
of new obedience, (Acts xi. 23.)   9) Restitution of things
ill-gotten, (Ex. xxxiii. 14, 15. Lev. vi. 1—7. Luke xix.
8, 9.)—10) Forgiveness of things which our neighbours
have committed against us,—(Matt. vi. 14, 15.)   11) Works
of mercy or alms.   Which how much they avail to obtain
remission of sins from God, is sufficiently clear from that
well-known passage, Dan. iv. 27. where the holy prophet
suggests this wholesome counsel to king Nebuchadnezzar,
as yet sticking fast in his sins, ' Redeem thy sins by
almsgiving and thine iniquities by shewing mercy to the
poor.'—Herewith agreeth in the New Testament what
St. James teacheth in this same 2d chapter, v. 13. ' Judgment without mercy to him, who hath shewed no mercy.'
But what ' mercy' he means, is clear from what follows,
v. 15, 16.   See Luke xi. 41. (and Grotius on the place,
Is. i. 17. Luke xvi. 9. 1 Tim. vi. 17, &c. 1 Pet. iv. 8.
Heb. xiii. 16. so that Chrysostome truly said (in the
Sermon on repentance), ' Repentance without almsgiving

L

is dead and hath no wings.' And hence (to note this by the way) arose that practice observed in the ancient Church, whereby, of such as through very grave offences had fallen under the censure of the Church, there was required, to make them capable of absolution, not only confession of sins and amendment of their past life, but also works of mercy, by them called ἀγαθοεργίαι, good works. You see how widely works of repentance extend; you see that they are all laid down by the Holy Spirit as altogether necessary to obtain forgiveness of sins."

Since, then, repentance is a work or, as Bp. Bull says, " a complex of good works," and yet antecedent to justification, it follows that there are works, in their degree acceptable to God, by Whose aid and the inspiration of Whose good Spirit they are wrought, antecedent to a man's complete justification; whereas Bp. Bull's opponent, that he might escape admitting that works had any connection with justification, consistently maintained, that " repentance or true contrition for sin, was no ways necessary to obtain the first justification." Bp. Bull, in support of his doctrine, appeals to the Homilies, our Liturgy, and Catechism, that repentance (including the fruits of repentance), as well as faith, is requisite to justification; and Field", whom he quotes, declares in the name of the Protestants generally;

" They teach no such thing [as they were charged with by Stapleton, ' that they make our justification to consist in the sole remission of sins by faith, that the sacraments confer nothing to our justification]' but that Baptism and repentance are necessarily required in them that are to be first justified."

It is clear, then, that the object of our Articles was, to secure broadly the great principles, that we are accounted righteous before God, for the merits of our Redeemer, received through faith, not for our own ; that even when justified, our works, through the remains of corruption in us, cannot be the grounds of our final acceptance, as neither were those before justification, of our justification ; in few words, that we were chosen beforehand, of God's free grace, not on account of any thing in us, to be made members of His Son ; and when in Him, are finally accepted, for His sake, in Whom we are.   The doctrine, which it would exclude by Art. xiii., is a form of Pelagianism, that the works in themselves " make men meet to receive grace," that God chooses men to the privileges of the Gospel with regard to what they, by their natural powers, became : the statement, of course, does not mean to exclude the truth, that " grace used attracts more grace ;" that " to him that hath, shall be given ;" that obedience to God's fainter and indistincter calls is rewarded by Him by clearer and distincter, until " whom He hath called, them He also justifieth."

[m]   Dr. Th. Tull quoted in the Apol. pro Harm. sect. 7. §. 2.
[n]   App. to B. 3. on the Church, p. 298.

Our friend's words then seem to me fully borne out ;

"They[o] [the Articles] say that works before grace and justification are worthless and worse, and that works after grace and justification are acceptable, but they do not speak at all of works with God's aid before justification."

———

I have now gone through the several Articles, of which explanations were given in our friend's Tract ; I examined these explanations carefully, with a view to ascertain whether they did contain any relaxation of the Articles (as I myself understood them) or no ; had it appeared to me so, there was yet the further question, to what extent the Articles were meant to include persons, who did not go so far from doctrine existing in the Church of Rome as their Authors ; it is certain from Bp. Burnet's statement, quoted by our friend[p], that this was the object of a change in the 28th Article, when the 39 Articles were, in Q. Elizabeth's reign, formed out of the 42 ; to me, however, there seemed no occasion to go to this point ; I have felt no doubt, carefully and conscientiously examining both editions of the Tract, that the meaning in which our friend would have them construed, in conformity and subordination to the teaching of the Church Catholic, is not only *an* admissible, but *the* most legitimate, inter-

[o] Tract 90, p. 81.   [p] Tract 90, p. 82.

pretation of them; it appears to me as clear, that they are not directed against any thing occurring, here and there, in the early Church, even though not Catholic, but against the existing system in the Church of Rome. This appears to me so plain, that I cannot but think that any who persist in those imputations of " jesuitism, dishonesty, &c." must be actuated by some " spirit, they know not of." Nor need I conceal my deep regret, that a body, for whom we both feel much respect and regard, should, in this instance, have departed from its wonted caution and tenderness of proceeding, and condemned precipitately, unexplained and unheard, the principles of the Tract, which, so suddenly brought before them, they but imperfectly understood. On a former occasion when you were away from us, they suspended, for a whole Term, the proposed condemnation of a publication, in order to give time for the Author to explain his views, and for that explanation to be weighed; on the present, they thought it better not to wait even two days. They admitted that they had no precedent upon which to proceed; but they preferred, in all this haste, to establish a new one. I do not mean to impute any personal unkindness to them; quite the contrary; some of them (deceiving themselves, I must think) thought that they were doing what was kindest towards our friend, by precipitating the condemnation of the Tract, while he was yet induced by the wishes of friends to withhold his name; I only mean to express what is generally felt, that they acted under panic and excitement, produced by misconception and misrepresentation. They could not, I think, have judged as they did, had they allowed the first alarm and excitement to pass by, had they heard (as they were requested from more than one quarter, and from one which they ought most to have regarded) the explanation which was all but on the point of being laid before them, and " given the accused license to answer for himself concerning the crime laid against him." It is grievous certainly that the Heads of Houses should, on so imperfect a view of the case, have encouraged by their authority, all the imputations of dishonesty so freely cast upon us, because we understand our Church and her system in a way different from one, of late popular among persons, who, we must think, have very little studied either her, her character, or her formularies. Not less embarrassing is the very vagueness and comprehensiveness of their condemnation ; " interpretations, such as are suggested in the Tract;"—*all* such are condemned ; yet what they are, is left for each to gather for himself as best he may ; one will claim the authority of the Board [b] for one thing, one for another,

---

[b] Even such a writer as Dr. Miller, gives circulation to the report, that the " Board of the University" had " actually instituted the appeal [to the Church] which he [Dr. M.] had resolved to prefer, in the transmission of a most obnoxious Tract

as each may be disposed; while I myself, and those who look on the Tract as I do, can only think that they condemned '' modes of interpretation,'' which they inferred to be contained in it, but which never had any real existence.   I should be sorry needlessly to say any thing which might pain a body, whom I much value, and from whom I hope much ; yet I cannot but think that they have put themselves in a false position, condemning unheard the Tract of one, over whom they had no authority, and that in terms so vague as readily to admit of being stretched to what I am convinced they did not intend, the '' mode of interpretation'' really contemplated in the Tract, the Catholic interpretation of the Articles and the Catholic scheme of doctrine.   I may as well speak out what is commonly felt; I cannot but think that, along with any anxiety about the danger of '' modes of interpretation'' of the Tract, which I have ground to think had been inculcated very earnestly upon them, they were under an unconscious bias, that they wished to relieve the University of the onus of the Tracts, as much as to condemn any '' modes of interpretation;'' and that the preamble '' the

of which Mr. N. had acknowledged himself the writer, to the several Bishops of the English Church.'' (Letter to Prof. Sewell, Irish Eccl. Journ. No. 10.)   A private individual did send the Tract, on his own responsibility, to the Bishops of England and Ireland, and this is made the act of the Board of Heads of Houses, and that Board the '' Board of the University.''

Tracts for the Times, a series of anonymous publications purporting to be written by Members of
the University, *but which are in no way sanctioned
by the University itself*," was as important in their
eyes, as the resolution which it ushered in.   Certainly, unless this had been a prominent object
with them, there was no occasion for so designating
the Tracts at all, and it is difficult to imagine in
what way the University could have been supposed
to have " sanctioned" Tracts, over which it had no
control, which were not even printed within it, did
not bear its " Imprimatur," did not any way fall
under its statutes or its cognizance.   On the other
hand, while they condemned this Tract on the
ground of a statute, enjoining " that every student
shall be instructed and examined in the 39 Articles
and shall subscribe to them ;" they left uncon-
demned a " History of Christianity" by one also
a member and once a Professor in the University,
which in a very distressing way explains away
miracles of our Blessed Lord ; and yet, that same
statute enjoins, that every student be instructed and
examined in the *" Evidences of religion :"* they had
recently listened very patiently to a sermon denying
Baptismal regeneration.   I do not question their
right to disconnect the University from the Tracts
in question, although it was done rather by a side-
wind ; we never sought to compromise the University, nor to gain its sanction ; we are but what we
are, private individuals in it, formed by her teach-

ing, by the spirit which she breathes, by the moral tone which her discipline imparts ; her sons, and the sons of those who transmitted these doctrines to us.   But now that they have formally disclaimed " any way sanctioning the Tracts" and have relieved the University of this odium, and disembarrassed her defence by her " friends without," I own I think it would be but befitting their candour, to reconsider the whole subject, qualify (if on mature thought they see occasion) the sentence which they lately passed, and state more definitely what they object to, what they do not.   This they are called upon to do by others[c], in an opposite direction, and to make their condemnation more stringent.   I fear nothing from the real expression of their opinion, such as it would now be formed, after the interval of peace and calm which the Holy Season, lately past, brought with it.

I would now, only, in conclusion, say a few words on two subjects incidentally connected with the Tract ;—the acknowledged tendency of certain individuals in our Church to Romanism, and the position of our own Church.

[c] The Edinburgh Review, No. 147, p. 293. which very consistently urges as a ground, that on the supposed principles of Tract 90, Dissenters would be admissible to the University ; which, of course, it must much deprecate !

Of the extent of the tendency to Romanism, which our friend acknowledges to exist in detached cases, I have no means of forming any estimate ; but, whatever it be, it is surely a very short-sighted view to make the Tracts or their authors responsible for it. Was not the Church warned sixteen years ago, (when we were being taught, not teaching,) by that teacher whose memory we together cherish and revere, " with very solemn seriousness," to " buckle on her armour and prepare herself to defend her very citadel and the palladium of her faith ?" Were there no secessions to Romanism before the Tracts began ? none, and not rather in large numbers, and those wholly persons whose Church-views were most opposed to our's ? In Edinburgh alone, the annual converts to Romanism were calculated at 100 ; but from the Kirk, not from our Church. No! Rome has many sympathies whereby to draw persons to herself. To those who would lean, she offers undoubting guidance ; for those who would have certainty, she offers infallibility ; for the devout, she has her Churches ever open and her frequent public services, her retreats for devotion and contemplation ; for the affectionate, she has the memory of the saints of old ; for the imaginative, she has a nominal reverence for Antiquity and a visible Unity of Communion, spread over the whole

* British Critic, No. 1. 1825.

world, and every where professing to teach the same truth. Her theory of Unity (to speak of this first) at once fills the imagination and contents the intellect. It is indeed a saltus mortalis; but those who can shut their eyes and take it, it places beyond further difficulty. The visible unity of the Church falls short of what it should be and what we should have hoped; Rome cuts the knot by maintaining that her one Communion is the one Church. Her's is indeed a fearful theory, cutting off at one stroke 90 millions of the Greek Orthodox Church, as well as our own Communion. Yet, if any shrink not from this, or know not that there is a Church as large almost as that of Rome, which she cuts off from the Church " out of which there is no salvation," in order to make way for her scheme, it is a simple theory: it removes all the difficulties which these sad and long rents of the Church present to other theories of her Unity, to say boldly with Rome, that the Church is visibly one still; that intercommunion is essential to the one visible Church; that Rome and Churches not in communion with her cannot form one Church; that the Churches in communion with Rome, as being the majority of Christendom, are the Church; and that therefore Churches, not in communion with her, are no Churches. In this way, any strong statement of the claims and the unity of the Church may be made a ground for joining the Romish communion, and I myself know a case, in which this effect was produced by some tracts of the Christian Knowledge Society.

Again, to take another class of minds, long residence at Rome, now so common with our countrymen, cannot be a thing indifferent; what is Catholic and un-Catholic is so strangely blended together in the Roman system, that if what is un-Catholic repels not, what is Catholic must win; the German artists have continually been drawn to her through their studies; among our own people, it is well known that the associations with the bright early days of the Faith, with Apostles and Martyrs, the richness of her worship, her solemn and primitive music, her paintings, her ceremonies, have again and again created a sympathy with her whole system, evil as well as good; it is idle then for persons to bring their families within the sphere of all which is fascinating to the senses in the Romish system, to take them to the ceremonies, with which, unless very well regulated or else profane, they will unduly sympathize, and then attribute to any publications in England the tendency to Romanism. Persons who had returned to this country, with a strong bias towards Rome, have been recovered by our teaching; their bias came not from us, but from the thoughtlessness which familiarized them with its mingled beauties and corruptions.

Again, another class is predisposed to Rome by the harsh language used towards her, and by careless imputations, which they discover to be unfounded [w] : another by the conflicting opinions among ourselves, which it sees to be unnatural and a defect in the state of a Church, and which it hopes to escape by giving itself up implicitly to one, who undertakes to guide it [x]. Another is attracted by her order and discipline ; another by the self-devotion of some of her members [y] ; another by finding in her, amid her corruptions, (which in this country are removed from sight,) Catholic truths and practices which they have never been taught to see, where they are, in their own Church. These hear, for the first time, in her, of the high doctrine of the

---

[w] " I can say for myself, and I think every one who advances from Protestantism towards Catholicity can say with me, that as light breaks upon our minds we do not doubt of Rome, our doubts lie the other way ; for we say Rome is right so far ; we have been deceived ; and being wrong in these points, there is reason to fear that we are wrong in others. We doubt Protestantism as a whole, and suspect that Rome is right." " Rev. Mr. Mason, a distinguished convert," quoted in Rev. J. Rathborne's [a Romanist] Letter on the Oxford Movement, p. 18. A person's bias ought to be to trust the Communion in which he was made a member of Christ ; but this writer, discovering himself to have been in error in some points as to another Communion, mistrusted his Church, and trusted Rome. In like way, the only person who went over to Rome, professing previously to have valued some of our writings, went over in about three weeks ; setting aside all other circumstances, what must be thought of that person's sense of responsibility, who, in three weeks after his first impression in favour of a foreign Communion, could decide on forsaking that in which God had placed him ?

[x] e. g. the authoress of the two first vols. of Geraldine.

[y] The sight of the sœurs de la charité has had this effect.

Holy Eucharist, while that of Transubstantiation is glossed over; and they think that in her alone, is the Holy Eucharist more than a sign or commemoration. They witness, in her, weekly fastings or daily prayers, and know not that their own Church enjoins the one, and provides the other; that the negligence of the laity in coming, alone hinders the daily service being realized as our Church desires. They hear, in her, that almsdeeds are good for the soul, and have not been taught the comforts of almsgiving, which our Communion Service sets forth in the words of Holy Scripture, and our Homilies from its teaching, in connection with the fathers. They hear of the value of habitual confession of sins before God's ministers, as a means of self-discipline, and of the benefits of Absolution, and know not that our Church suggests it for such as need it, and leaves them at liberty to choose for their Confessor whom they will [z]. In these and in other ways, it has continually happened that persons have sought in the Communion of Rome, what was laid up for them in their own, more fully and without corruption, had they but known it; and this valuable class will, of course, be the more secured from wandering, the more the high Catholic

---

[z] " Let him come unto me, or to some other discreet and learned Minister of God's Word, and open his grief; that by the ministry of God's holy Word, he may receive the benefit of absolution," &c. First Exhort. in Communion Service.

doctrines of our Church are developed, and her principles acted on. Instances have recently occurred, in which by these means persons, for many years estranged from her communion, have been restored to it from that of Rome which they had joined. Again, the more people cast themselves back into Antiquity, and sympathize with the Fathers and the Saints of old, and feel themselves one Church with the Church of primitive times, the more will that painful void be filled up, which is caused by her present state of isolation. We have a communion of Saints, a fellowship of doctrine, a oneness by descent, with the Church in Apostolic days, even if those who are now in the flesh acknowledge us not.

The character also in which Rome exhibits herself in England, much aggravates our present difficulties ; her policy is a corruption of the Apostolic wisdom, to '' become all things to all, that by all means, it may" gain some ; '' it falleth down and humbleth itself, that the congregations of the poor may fall into the hands of its strong ones.'' Her principle, that there is no salvation out of Communion with herself, makes it her first object to draw people any how into her Communion. The extent too of her Communion is the tangible proof she puts forward of her being *the* Catholic Church. This is a sore temptation to her to bend, relax, fall in with unholy ways and usages, which promote this her first end. She would further, holiness as much as she can; but she cannot afford to do what is right, if it would cause the unholy to part from her. She is obliged to temporize, to lure, to condescend, when she cannot control. In some countries she is suffering the penalty of former sins, having to support the credit of false miracles; which she cannot disavow, without owning the past to have been a fraud; while in all, over which she has dominion, she will tolerate and profit by what she dares not approve; will sit by in silence while men tell falsehood or use violence in her behalf; will suffer visions and miracles which she does not believe, to be believed by her people and to bring gain to her clergy; and even in her own guarded province of the faith will permit unauthorized doctrines (such as that of the immaculate Conception) to creep in and take the public honours of truth[h], wherever men are disposed to receive them. It is painful to think and speak of these things in another member of the mystical Body of Christ, who once was the bulwark of the Faith and a pattern of zeal, and who still has holy practices and institutions, which we might gladly imitate; but Rome forces it upon us by sending amongst us to steal away the hearts of the children of our Church, boldly denying whatever corruptions our people have not before their eyes; since these things were swept away by the Reformation, and she has been able to begin anew

[h] Festivals and Churches in honour of it.

in a spirit more congenial to that of religious minds here, and more approximating to early Christianity. Thus for the more "enthusiastic feelings of foreign hearts[i]," where the presence of a Reformed Church furnishes no check, she has wonder-working images of the Blessed Virgin curiously decked out, through the offerings of those taught to seek relief from them[k]; rival images, which for some time contended for superiority through the cures which they were alleged to perform, until at last popular favour having turned towards the one[l], it receives all the offerings, the other remains neglected and in disgrace; pictures of saints which are said, by being carried

---

[i] Dr. Wiseman, Letter to Mr. Newman, p 25. These feelings, I am assured, meet with but partial sympathy, and sometimes with wonder and doubt, amongst Romanists of our own country who are sojourners abroad.

[k] It is but following the example of Dr. Wiseman (p. 26.) to give the following recent dialogue between an earnest-minded English Catholic traveller and the person who shewed the Church; " In a Church at Venice (I am as sure as I can be it was the del Camine) I saw a Madonna gorgeously dressed, and asked why it was so unusually decorated. The Sagrestano said, It was ' a very rich Madonna,' and that the people brought every year great offerings of oil, wax, and money. I asked why? He said, ' it had done many miracles.' I said, ' I know God could do miracles, but did not understand how an image should do miracles.' He said, ' The Madonna prays for us in Heaven.' I said, ' Supposing that to be so, I see no connection between her intercession, and this image of wood and silk.' He said, ' The faith teaches us so.' "

[l] That in the Augustinian Church, in Rome; the other is in the Pantheon.

M

in procession, to have stopped the plague and
to have averted the Cholera ; at Rome, the image
of a " Holy Child" is brought forth to bless
the people, and much benefit looked for by the
populace from its blessing and the honour paid to
it[m] ; at Naples the blood of S. Januarius is still
yearly liquefied[n], and the people are encouraged to
look upon the imposture as the sign of the favour
of the Almighty[o] ; in another Church is a waxen
figure of our Lord as an infant, to which the king
and the Court make an annual procession at
Christmas, the king carrying scissors to cut the
hair of the image, which, it is asserted, grows
miraculously every year[p] ; at Rome is an image of the
Virgin which on one day in the year nods her head

[m] It is kept in the Church of the Ara Cœli in the Capitol.
Popular stories are told of its return to the Church, after it had
been sent for to work a cure, and another been exchanged for it,
too painfully ludicrous to set down, considering Whom the
image represents.

[n] A corresponding imposture and the mode of its being
wrought at Hales in Gloucestershire, is related by Bp. Burnet,
Hist. Ref. b. iii. t. i. p. 441.

[o] " The scenes said often to take place on the Festival of S.
Januarius almost exceed belief ; if the blood liquefies quickly, all
the people praise the Saint and promise him offerings ; if not,
they abuse him in most unmeasured terms, (some of which were
repeated to me,) and threaten not to send him any more gifts,
or to take any more notice of him." Statement of a traveller.
It has been an habitual practice to delay the apparent liquefying
of the blood and ascribe it to the presence of " heretics"
(English persons).

[p] Statement of a traveller.

when she grants prayers[q]; the Church is thronged to see it; indulgences are still granted for visiting favourite shrines[r]; in Italy, the prayers which

[q] Burnet has a similar account, Hist. Ref. b. iii. t. i. p. 440, 1. "For their images, some of them were brought to London, and were there, at St. Paul's Cross, in the sight of all the people, broken; that they might be fully convinced of the juggling impostures of the monks. And in particular, the crucifix of Boxley in Kent, commonly called *the rood of grace;* to which many pilgrimages had been made, because it was observed sometimes to bow, and to lift itself up; to shake, and to stir head, hands, and feet; to roll the eyes, move the lips, and bend the brows: all which were looked on by the abused multitude as the effects of a divine power. These were now publicly discovered to have been cheats: for the springs were showed, by which all these motions were made. Upon which John Hilsey, then Bishop of Rochester, made a sermon, and broke the rood in pieces." A similar story of " a wooden image of the Virgin, held in very great veneration, bowing its head in acknowledgment of salutations, and stretching forth a finger, which before was doubled," together with a miraculous voice, is gravely told in a short " treatise on the most famous confraternity of the Scapular." Dublin.

[r] The following copies of Indulgences are furnished by the traveller alluded to, note k.

1. In the Church of S. Cosmo e Damiano in the Forum at Rome.

Indulgence.

" The image (picture) of the most holy Mary which is at the great altar spoke to the Pope St. Gregory, and said to him, ' Why dost thou not salute me in passing as thou wert wont?' The Saint asked pardon, and granted to those that should celebrate mass at that altar, the liberation of a soul from Purgatory, that is, of that soul for which the mass is celebrated."

2. In the Church of S. Maria Sopra Minerva, Rome, under

M 2

occur in the middle of the sermon, seem often studiously directed to the Blessed Virgin ; in the South of France, the Jesuits are now anew directing the devotions of the poorer people to the Blessed Virgin ; in Ireland, it is taught that the wearing of the Scapular of the Virgin, which may be lined with silk, saves from Hell^q, and that on performance

the short exercise in honour of the afflicted heart of the most holy Mary.

Sacra Indulgenza.

" His Holiness our Lord Pope Pius VII. fel. req. vouchsafed to grant for ever the indulgence of 300 days, applicable to the holy souls in Purgatory, to all the faithful every time they shall recite the above prayers, according to the Rescript dated January 3, 1825."

3. Also over the entrance to the Chapel of Santa Maria della Salute.

" His Holiness our Lord Pope Gregory XVI. by a brief dated September 17, 1836, accorded a plenary indulgence to whomsoever, after confessing and communicating, shall devoutly visit this holy image of the blessed Virgin under the title of Consolatrice degli afflitti, on the second Sunday in July and its octave in every year. He conceded also the partial indulgence of 200 days to whomsoever, at least contrite, shall visit the same holy image on any day of the year. The above indulgences are moreover applicable to the good of the souls in Purgatory.

February 11, 1839.

4. In the Medici Chapel at San Lorenzo, Florence.

Paulus V. Pont. Max. cuique Sacerdoti qui ad hoc altare pro defunctis litaverit, animam *supremis pœnis* liberare perpetuo, AN. MDCX. concessit."

See further on Indulgences Mr. Palmer's First Letter to Dr. Wiseman, p. 16—19, 31, 2. 43. and above, p. 91. note k.

^q " If our blessed Lady had bid us do some great thing, we ought to do it ; how much rather then when she saith, Wear

of some easy conditions, she delivers those of the Confraternity from Purgatory on the first Saturday after their decease[r]; at Rome the month of May is annually devoted to her service and called by her name; her medal or picture is solemnly placed on the breasts of children; the declaration of her power and compassion is held, in spiritual exercises, to be efficacious, even with sinners who have listened unmoved to arguments from the justice and mercy of God; her name seems often to displace that of the Third Person of the Blessed Trinity; she is still held

---

my livery and you shall not suffer eternal fire! If she had enjoined us to make a great abstinence; to undergo some rigorous mortification; or to undertake a long and tedious pilgrimage, with this condition, that we should be freed from eternal damnation; from the torments of purgatory, and from the many dangerous events which easily do befal us in this life; right reason would dictate to us, that we ought to attempt any thing for the obtaining of so great good: how much more then, when she had annexed these and many more extraordinary graces to the reception only, and devout wearing the holy habit of the Scapular, with a final confidence in her powerful protection; but you will, perhaps, with Naaman, object, what can such a weak thing avail us, as the Scapular is? To this I answer with the apostle, (1 Corinth. i. 27.) The weak things of the world hath God chosen, that he might confound the strong. He that made choice of the weak element of water to wash us from the original sin, which is deeply indicated in us by the prevarication of our first father Adam, hath made use of the weak habit of the Scapular to produce those excellent effects which are mentioned in the chapter following.

[r] Treatise on the Scapular, c. 9. (Dublin.)

out virtually as a preferable mediatrix to our Lord Himself[s], and popular feeling flows so directly towards adoration of her, that even Rome herself has at least on one occasion been forced to pause and has denied to her image, what it is shocking should ever have been asked for it[t],—honours hitherto reserved for those mysteries in which Rome acknowledges the presence of God incarnate.   In the new school of art in Munich, on the contrary, where religion is in a purer form, the Mother, as in the oldest school[u], has again become a subordinate object, and although enthroned, is worshipping her Son.   In Ireland, Romanism becomes political and is subservient to demagogues ;   in the United States, she boasts that she is Republican ;   on the continent of Europe she courts absolute sovereigns ;   among ourselves, she drops, as far as possible, every thing distinctive, and assimilates herself, as much as may be, to the Anglican Church ;   " Transubstantiation" is represented as the doctrine of the " Real Presence ;" pictures of Purgatory, and Purgatorial societies have no place, and persons are allowed to believe Purgatory itself to be only the loss of the Divine

[s] See Postscript.
[t] viz. the use of the canopy in processions.
[u] In the oldest paintings, the Madonna is introduced, meditating on or praying to, or proposing for contemplation her Infant Son ; in the school of Raphael, &c. she is only shewing a mother's care, and, as the mother, is the chief object.

Presence (pœna damni), not any sensible suffering (pœna sensus), and so to differ little from the doctrine of the intermediate state[x]; (while in Ireland persons are incited to religious acts in memory of The Passion of our Lord by the grant of indulgences, many plenary, others for many hundred years[y], "applicable to *suffering* souls in Purgatory.") Invocations of Saints, in which they are called upon themselves to aid us, are withdrawn, and the practice is represented as identical with requests to friends on earth[z]; Indulgences are limited

[x] One, who had gone over to Romanism, stated to the Author that he had never met with any other doctrine as to Purgatory, among Romanists, though he had spoken with very many. The pain, according to him, consisted in an intense longing for the Divine Presence; so that, instead of being a state of " greater suffering than any thing in this life," (see above, p. 84—87,) it would be a state of higher joy than is vouchsafed to most Christians, corresponding to that spoken of in the Canticles.

[y] " The pious sodality," &c. p. 80. see above, p. 92. note k. In Bouvier, the word " suffering" does not occur. Again in the treatise on the Scapular, c. 7. " The excellency and greatness of this privilege [the speedy release of the souls of the confraternity through S. Mary] will easily appear, if we consider how horrible the *broiling* torments of purgatory are ; (the angelical doctor S. Thomas saith) that they do exceed the pains, which Jesus Christ suffered in His holy Passion.—From these fearful torments the devouts of the holy Scapular are exempted, &c."

[z] Dr. Wiseman admits, " Without wishing to cast censure upon any one, I have observed with pain, that occasionally in controversy regarding the Saints and their Queen, there is a temptation to lower the consideration in which we hold them,

to the remission of punishment on this earth; " images and pictures" are become again only "instruments of teaching," or reminiscences of absent friends. " These things," said Romanist ecclesiastics from our country in the presence of one of the favourite images at Rome, " seem strange to us." " They carry the worship of the Blessed Virgin and of the Saints too far here; it interferes with the worship of God." In Italy, miracles are alleged on authority, in support of doctrine, which, in this country are withdrawn [a] from the narrative, as suspicious or unbefitting.   Among us, as (in the main) a

to dim their glory, and perhaps to save ourselves some re-proaches, at the expense of our Catholic brethren abroad." Remarks on Mr. Palmer's Letter, end.   Dr. W. perhaps does not know, as we do, that in our countrymen of his Communion, these feelings of disparagement of their brethren abroad are not assumed only in controversy, but are often seriously enter-tained.

[a] " I read it [the original of Liguori's " Glories of Mary," approved of by the Convocation of Rites, with the sanction of Pius VII. 1803.] most carefully, and was surprised to find that the main proofs for this unscriptural worship was a series of visions and supposed miracles said to be wrought by images, &c. almost all of them childish beyond conception, and some of them ludicrous in the extreme.   On comparing the translation with the original, I found that the translator had prudently sup-pressed the most silly."   Rev. E. Nixon, Address to the Roman Catholic Inhabitants of Castletown, 1840.   The author, who writes only in self-vindication, abstains from translating these stories, because " I do not like trifling upon any religious sub-ject, and it would be impossible to read those fables with a grave countenance."

moral earnest people, Confession is used as a check to sin; in Italy the obligation to it is made consistent with a state of society generally and openly charged with the grossest profligacy, tempting to it, and in itself almost implying the commission of " adultery in the heart ;" if common opinion be but partially grounded in truth, we must believe that adulterers and adulteresses receive absolution from the Priest, and " return to their vomit" which they never purposed to quit : while in Rome which calls itself " Mater Orbis" the first Bishop of the West presides over a government chiefly composed of Ecclesiastics, and yet so corrupt that it has passed into a proverb that the sight of Rome is incompatible with faith, " Roma veduta, fede perduta." In this country, fasting is dispensed with on account of sickness only ; in Spain dispensations from fasting, except on Friday, are sold, as a matter of course, to any one, or to whole families habitually, who prefer not to fast ; in Rome, the very Day of our Lord's Passion (and that, during the very hours when He was nailed to the Cross for us) is uniformly, amid some outward distinctions of meats, made by Cardinals a day of official entertainment and a feast[b]. " When I go to

---

[b] " On Good Friday Cardinal ———— received all the Cardinals at dinner at two in the afternoon with many Englishmen in uniform. The dinner consisted of soup, fish, cutlets, and every variety of dish all made of fish, but indistinguishable

mass in my own country," said a pious German nobleman lately, " it is to pray; but here [at Rome] prayer seems the last object for which people assemble; the fashionable Churches are mere conversaziones." And while among us cor- ruptions are withdrawn, Rome adopts studiously " evangelical" language [c]; exhibits beautiful pic- tures of monastic life to attract the enthusiastic among us; introduces " orders of mercy" such as we might have ourselves, which we too need, and which are most calculated to win a kind- hearted nation. In this way, she has gained some, and is too likely to gain more; whether in the end she will not have to repay with usury those whom by such means she has gained, we cannot yet see; such converts are Anglicans at heart; at least are far nearer to our Communion, than (in its present state) to that to which they have joined themselves; this, as our Church realizes her position, they may, we trust, more and more see; their sympathies are with us, not with the corruptions in the Roman Church; we have resigned them, we trust, in chastisement only, to receive them again after a while, bringing back with them, (if it may be,)

from the richness of the sauces from any other dinner. This was annual." MS. Journal.

   [c] Such was the impression upon the author, on reading the 3d vol. of Geraldine; attributed to an able controversialist. The very vehicle, being unreal, (a story,) perhaps gave the more temptation to use unreal language; yet the same has been observed by another, who would " think no evil."

the rest of that estranged Communion to our
ancient British Church; we may hope that it is
but like the Eastern fable, that the darkness
greedily swallowed the light, but was itself overcome by that which it absorbed into itself. But
though we may hope this in the end, they who
join the Romish Communion in this country on
the ground of its purity from what is peculiarly
Romish, have no security that they may not at any
time be entangled in the whole system; what has
been, may again be; and one may unhesitatingly
say, that it is the presence of our Church alone, which
makes Romanism in this country so different from
what it was, and, in Italy especially, now is.
Whoever joins it from our Communion does what
in him lies to bring back that darkness, by
weakening the Church which mainly keeps it in
check; and, since their Communion is one, he
makes himself responsible for the corruption elsewhere prevailing; he countenances in others, what
in his own person he avoids.

But, besides these difficulties from without, there
will be, it must be added, others from within; a
system, practical and reverent, as is the true
Catholic system in our Church, tends more than
any other, by God's grace, to produce a sense of
responsibility in those who embrace it; still no
scheme of doctrine will in itself protect those
who hold it: in any extensive revival of doctrine,
truths will be very unequally received, and will

be perverted by those who do not receive them
in " an honest and true heart ;" some will take
them up as a beautiful theory, as matter of
imagination, and these " having no root in themselves," will " in time of temptation fall away ;"
others will embrace them with ardour and affection,
but without self-discipline and humility, and these
too, it is to be feared, secure that they are standing, and not " taking heed," will fall.   There are
many forms of unreality ; many ways in which
those who are unreal, may deceive themselves, and
seem to themselves wheat when they are but chaff ;
and, as being such, will be carried away out of the
barn-floor by the sifting wind of temptation, whenever it is permitted to blow upon them.   This the
writers of the Tracts cannot help; they may lament
to hear of persons allowing themselves in the habit
of speaking indignantly of sins committed at the
time of or in the English Reformation, instead
of humbling themselves for " their own sins and
the sins of their forefathers," and acknowledging that
what we have is more than we deserve, more than
we realize, is what is best fitted for us[l]; it is sad
to see or hear of persons, talking and not acting ;
fasting, as has been said, in theory and in their
studies[m] : it is sad to see people apparently prizing

---

[l] Tract 86. " Indications of a superintending Providence in
the preservation of the Prayer book, and in the changes which it
has undergone."

[m] Geraldine.

what is Catholic for its novelty not for its holiness; or tempting God, by approximating as near as they may to Romanism, and thinking that they shall not fall into it ; but surely it is responsibility enough, not directly to encourage any evil tendencies. Since men " wrest Scripture to their own damnation," how much more must the words of frail man be liable to abuse.

Those, also, who have been God's chief instruments in the great work of restoring half-forgotten doctrine,—I mean our friend himself, and the Author of the Christian Year,—have again and again repeated, that the change which is going on around us is " not[n] satisfactorily accounted for by any particular movement of individuals on a particular spot." They have declined the praise ; let them not unduly bear the blame. In part, we must all bear it ; no one can doubt that if the system of our Church were fully carried out, her doctrine fully taught, her holy precepts acted up to, her devotions offered " in spirit and in truth," her Communions frequent and frequented as she desires, her self-denying training followed,—in a word, if all the means of grace, of which she is made the channel, were realized as they ought, God's blessing would so rest upon us, that we should have nothing to fear for our Vine ; " they who pass by," would not then " pluck off her

[n] Mr. Newman's Letter to Dr. Jelf, p. 27. British Critic, No. 50. " State of religious Parties."

grapes;" she would then have such marks of holiness, that they who now "gather themselves together against her would fall unto her;" her children, of whom she has been bereaved, would be restored unto her; nay, she herself might be carried to a yet higher condition; the discipline, whose loss she laments, be restored; she might, besides the hidden saints formed by her holy training, have those also who should visibly be saints, tokens, even to the world, of God's sanctifying Presence in her, like those of old, who were termed "Apostles of the nations." In whatever degree she is not such, we have all, more or less, our share of guilt; our sins, our negligences, the coldness of our intercessions, our listlessness or untamed energy, our want of holiness—each of us may know the plague of his own heart—have all contributed to deprive her of God's intended blessing, and to keep her where she is.   Let us not then seek to excuse ourselves or cast the blame upon others; it is not to excuse my friends—much less myself who am least and last—that I have said even thus much, but lest " the truth" should be " evil spoken of;" let us not care where the blame lies in man's sight, but rather let us all seek, more and more, to " humble ourselves under the mighty hand of God, that He may exalt us in due time."

Such seems to me the position which one should wish for our whole Church; this does not seem to me to have been enough realized; the sensitiveness at some of our friend's strong language[n] on the actual condition of the Church implies this; we have been for some time on the defensive; we have been maintaining her character, as a pure and Apostolic Church, against the calumnies of men, rather than confessing before God, " for our sins, and for the iniquities of our fathers, Jerusalem and Thy people are become a reproach to all that are about us," and praying Him, " cause Thy Face to shine upon the sanctuary that is desolate, for the Lord's sake." To joy is more congenial than to weep; our natural love and piety towards her, as it makes us hope all good for her, and think all good of her, indisposes us to admit that there is any thing lacking to her; we think of her more, as God's Providence has formed her, than as by the remissness of our forefathers and our own, she has become; more of what she is in the abstract and in theory, than what she is, as a living, moving, acting, holy, Power, the depository of Divine graces and powers, destined not to struggle only with the world (as she is more and more) but to overcome it; not to have store of food only for such of her children as will receive it, but to bring them up, guide, restrain them; we think of the beautiful organization which her Lord has given her, that He has provided her with every thing needful for

---

[n] " Till her members are stirred up to this religious course, let the Church sit still; let her be content to be in bondage; let her work in chains;" &c. Tract, 90. p. 4.

all the functions of His body, and forget that through our sins she is in a state of powerlessness. His instrument still, yet not adequately performing the high destinies for which He formed, has again and again delivered, and yet preserves her.

Our true position seems to be, to acknowledge that we have fallen and that God is raising us up; amid much which is humbling, there are many cheering signs that the hand of God is with our Church; by looking exclusively on either side of the picture, we should risk forming a tone of mind, other than what is intended for us; we might be unduly elated, and forget our humility, or unduly depressed, and forget God's mercy. Our vine has been " burnt with fire and cut down," but " its branch is" again " tender and putting forth leaves," and giving signs of an approaching summer. Our Heathen populations; the extent of schism among us; fresh and fresh divisions, drawing away some of our more earnest members; our internal disunion, paralyzing our efforts, and wasting our energies; the fewness of those who share in works of piety or charity; our greediness of gain in order to minister to our luxuries; the indifference about holy things openly professed; the absence of any high standard or dislike to it; the appalling strides of a lawless infidelity; these and much besides are saddening proofs of a past and present winter; but the source of our hopes is not in ourselves; we seem ice-bound, but " He bloweth with His Spirit, and the

waters flow ;" the clods of our valleys seem yet
hard, but " He maketh it soft with the drops of
rain, and blesseth the increase of it ;" our hope is
not in ourselves nor in men ; but that the Lord of
the Vineyard is " looking down" graciously " from
heaven, beholding, and visiting this Vine, and the
vineyard which His right hand planted, and the
branch which He made strong for Himself,' and
that it is He Who is " sending out her boughs unto
the sea, and her branches unto the river."   A high
destiny seems to be yet in store for our Church ; it
is for her sake, we may hope, that her and our
people are being carried into every corner of the
world : certainly, to contrast her state, as she was
towards the close of last century, without a single
Bishop, out of these Islands, and as she now is
every where in possession of her complete Apostolic constitution, though not in the degree she
needs it, yet as centres from which she may spread,
one has ground to hope that the " multiplying of
the people" is to " increase her joy ;" her Bishops
shortly will be in every continent as well as in the
isles afar off ; her Episcopate (notwithstanding the
sore blow which cut off her Irish Bishoprics) is already
more than doubled ; she is not dwindling, as sects
after a time do, but growing ; in the United States
she has been quadrupled, while the population has
doubled ; she is there recognized even by those without her, as the only principle of stability in their land ;
hearts are turned unto her ; some she has gathered

N

in ; and it seems only a question of time, when the severed bodies shall be gathered into her, and it shall be seen, when she shall have enfolded the rest within her, which is indeed Moses' rod and given by God, which the formation of man; every step is an earnest of the final issue ; it seems already to be felt extensively among them, that she alone is the bulwark against Romish errors, and they seem to be preparing to take refuge under her shadow.

And with this outward extension, she is every where giving signs of life ; life in different forms, some regular, some irregular, more or less imperfect, yet still life ; every where her members seem more alive to her true character, and so, we may trust, will more act up to it ; and zeal, which has hitherto so often sought a vent without her, will be concentrated within her, and devote itself, in some allowed way, to remedy the great wants of our people ; her prayers and Communions are again becoming more frequent ; in some places, her two days of humiliation, her Litany days ; elsewhere daily ; her Communions are weekly in some places where they were monthly, and monthly Communions are becoming the ordinary provision even for her village Congregations ; and with increased Communions, they who partake of them are increased also, and there is increased faith and sense of their value, and so, we may trust again, fresh life poured into the Church from the Fountain of life ; her Lents and weekly fasts are more

observed, " self-denial (fasting) and almsgiving,
the wings of prayer," are growing; her care for
Christ's lambs, her thought of Christ's poor,
(deficient as it yet is,) are increasing; there is
(as you will have witnessed in this place) a more
devout, an humbler spirit than heretofore, even at
that most trying period of human life; the deposit
of our Faith is more reverenced; there is a yearn-
ing after the holy days of the Church's " first"
virgin " love ;" our very divisions, we may hope,
are marks of earnestness; persons whom I cannot
but think to be partially in error, are in reality
contending not for the error but for the truth,
which is in their minds bound up with it, not against
truth, but against some error which they have
identified with others' statement of the truth.
What God is preparing us for, for doing or for
suffering, He only knoweth; yet one cannot but
hope that He is preparing us for something;
Romanists and Protestants alike have their eyes
upon our Church; who knows but that for us
may be reserved the office of " turning the hearts
of the fathers to the children, and of the children
to the fathers?" A thoughtful Romanist, lately,
even when speaking against foreign Protestants,
anticipated that if the Church were ever to be
again one, it must be through our's, " which being
both Catholic and Reformed, had her hands upon
both." Only " it is not for" us " to know the
times or the seasons which The Father hath put

in His own power ;" much less to anticipate them. Enough that we " see our signs ;" and that " the way in which we should go" is " made plain before our face." " A thousand years is with the Lord as one day," and He can make one day do the work of a thousand years. We have our office plainly marked out for us, (as has been often said,) to labour to act up to the principles of our Church, and to lead others to do the same ; so shall we be formed, and aid (under the Divine grace) to form others in the mould, of " godliness, righteousness, and soberness of life," provided in her ; we have but to seek to form ourselves and others in His holy Faith and the keeping of His commandments, and commit our Church and ourselves to Him, to deal with us, as in His Infinite Mercy He may vouchsafe. I cannot but hope, that they too, whose minds have been, from whatever cause, unsettled and tending to Romanism, will yet be stayed, and seeing the hand of God with our Church, " abide, wherein they have been called, with God," and forsake not the Church in which they were baptized, but await the end. Change from any Church is an act of solemn responsibility; much more would it be from one, to which, as our friend has developed, God has given the notes of " possession, freedom from party-titles, life, ancient descent, unbroken continuance, agreement in doctrine with the ancient Church* ;" much more

* British Critic, No. 53. Catholicity of the English Church.

still, when God's hand is visibly with her. To
leave her at such a time might be a very wilful and
presumptuous act, going, as far as man's wilfulness
can, to oppose the Divine counsels and defeat His
good purposes; it may be, perhaps, again true,
'' except these abide in the ship, ye cannot be
saved.'' One must fear too, lest such, voluntarily
foregoing the full use of the Holy Eucharist, as it
is vouchsafed to them in their own Church, might
provoke God to lessen His grace, as rejecting His
Gifts. But, as I said, let us act up to the
principles of our Church, and these brethren, who,
from whatever excuse, have been allowed thus to
be tempted of Satan to forsake the Church wherein
God placed them, will be in less risk of being
led into sin; their mother will not have to lament
the loss of those whom she has nourished up and
who may be valuable children to her.

It may be long ere the issue comes; at present,
the course pointed out to the several Churches
seems to be to amend themselves, to become again
what they once were, even though imperfect; to
'' return to their first deeds;'' so may they,
through repentance and amendment of life, and
keeping the commandments, be led to further
knowledge of the truth, and in the end be restored
to unity, if this blessing be yet in store for the
Church. At least such seems the course which
things, under God's guidance, are taking. Thus
even the Greek Church is again become pro-

selytizing; the Gallican Church is sending out Missionaries and praying for our conversion, shewing her new life, in part, in seeking to extend her own Communion; in Prussia, religion is reviving in connection with Lutheran doctrine; we are being guided back to the principles of our Church; we seem thus to be taught, as our friend concisely said, that " we are to go back, not to go over;" repentance and zeal must come first, union afterwards; union is to be looked for, as God's gift, to be prayed for, not compassed by man's device; " it is God that maketh men to be of one mind in a house:" our duties then lie not now towards Rome; our present path and duties are plain;—with ourselves; to fit ourselves to be His instrument: how we may be employed, when fitted, we cannot foresee and so should not forestall; it may be that our first office will be, not with Rome, but with those bodies which were separated from Rome at the same time as ourselves, but were not so signally blessed and preserved; it may be, that through us what is lacking in them to the full gifts of a Church is to be supplied; it may be, that " our light shining before men," they are thus to be led to " glorify our Father which is in Heaven;" and thus we may be reunited with the rest of Christendom, not alone nor selfishly, but decked with the rich jewelry of them whom we have won back to Primitive Faith and Discipline. It may be too the very way, in which it may please God, that the rest of the Church Catholic should be brought to love and respect, and seek to be one with, us, that we have aided to restore to Catholicity those who have gone away from it. Our office then is with ourselves and within ourselves, ready to do acts of charity to those severed from us, as far as we may without compromise, but not seeking untimely union. Such schemes have been baffled before, when things seemed most favourable, and so, a mark set upon them. As unity is perhaps a means to the greater holiness of the whole Church, so also holiness may be a condition of the restoration of unity. Let us act up to the principles of our Church, and realize her worship, her fastings, her repentance, her humiliations, her praise, her intercessions, her high standard of holy life, her exalted charity ; live up to what is evidently Catholic in her ; develope, as occasion requires, those Catholic points, which, though she has them, do not lie upon the surface ; in a word, be raised to what our Church should be ; and who knows but that He Who raises us up, may purify Rome too, and St. Peter be the type of the Church of St. Peter, and her Lord yet cast His gracious look upon her, and she weep bitterly her fall, and she, being "converted, strengthen" her "brethren," and deserve to be restored to the preeminence, which while she deserved, she had ; and the Western Church be reunited, not on any plan of human wisdom, of compromise or concession, but in holiness

and Primitive Faith? Who knows, again, whether it may not be His gracious will to re-
unite His whole Church at once, and why should
we then direct our eyes to the Western Church
alone, which, even if united in itself, would yet
remain sadly maimed, and sadly short of the Oneness she had in her best days, if she continued
severed from the Eastern? After a long separation,
in which we have not been known by name to the
Eastern Church, much less our real character, God
seems again to be opening to us ways of kindly
intercourse with some portions of her, which must
increase love, which will also, under God's blessing,
help her to restore the holiness and knowledge of her
early years, and therewith, make her wish to understand us better, and be united to us. All union of our
distracted Christendom " is impossible with man;
with God" it is as " possible," (and one may add
it may be as likely to be His will,) to unite His
whole Church in one, at once, whenever His time
may be, as any single portions of it. We pray
that God would " have mercy upon all Jews,
Turks, Infidels, and Heretics, and fetch them home
to His flock, that they may be saved among the
remnant of the true Israelites, and be made one
fold under One Shepherd:" why not hope, as we
also continually pray, that the whole Church also
may visibly become such a fold? that God would
" inspire His universal Church with the spirit of
truth, unity, and concord?" Such longings, (ac-

cording to the heads of good Bishop Andrews'
daily intercession,) for the good estate of the
" Church Catholic; Eastern; Western; our own,"
as they set before us a nobler end, so are they
more accordant with our Church's feelings as
expressed in her Liturgy, and they are safer.   The
Church Catholic can only be re-united on Catholic
principles ; the very thought and longing carries
us back to her pure days and her Œcumenical
Councils, and primitive faith and holiness ; it
awakens our sympathies only for an object upon
which they may rest without risk.   On the other
hand, longing for re-union with any branch of the
Church, as the Roman, naturally tends to make
man gloss over the difficulties, and shut their eyes
to the actual corruptions, which we should now be
called upon to recognise or to sanction ; it creates
sympathies not for her, as she once was, a " pure
Virgin," but for her very defilements : the very fact,
that it seems more within the compass of human
means, tends to make men impatient of hindrances,
which it seems as though God had placed, and desirous
to remove them or set them aside in an unholy way.
Let us long, not for what may be brought about by
a mere blending of our own practical unholiness
and short-comings with the corruptions of another
Church, thereby to aggravate in the sight of God
the very offensiveness of what is severally amiss in
us ; but rather let us long for what, being evidently
beyond the reach of man's device, leads us at once

to the throne of God, thence to expect it from the Great Head of the Church as He would give it, in holiness and holy love. We know not what may be, and so our duty is the easier, not to act as though we knew it ; rather to " do with all our might what our hand" now " findeth to do," not to run before, but to follow after ; not to plan or devise for ourselves, but to act where God leads. Be we zealous, earnest, patient, humble ; " He Who cometh will come, and will not tarry ;" and it may be, " His kingdom" will sooner " come," if we in our Church follow His gracious guidance.

May God give us grace, in these difficult days, more and more " perfectly to know His Son Jesus Christ to be the Way, the Truth, and the Life, that following the steps of His holy Apostles—we may stedfastly walk in the way that leadeth to eternal life, through the same His Son Jesus Christ our Lord."

Ever your very affectionate Friend,

E. B. PUSEY.

Christ Church,
Feast of S. Philip and S. James,
1841.

APPENDIX.

NOTE A. *page* 109.

Archbishop Ussher on the difference between ancient and modern Invocation of Saints, from his Answer to a Jesuit's Challenge, p. 445 sqq.

"—That we may the better understand, and more distinctly apprehend, how far the recommending of men's selves unto the prayers of the Saints, which began to be used in the latter end of the fourth age after Christ, came short of that invocation of Saints, which is at this day practised in the Church of Rome: these special differences may be observed betwixt the one and the other.

"First, in those elder times, he that prayed silently was thought to honour God in a singular manner; as one that ' brought [a] faith with him, and confessed that God was the searcher of the heart and reins and heard his prayer, before it was poured out of his mouth;' the understanding of the present secrets of the heart, by the general judgment of the Fathers, being [b] no more communicated by Him unto the creatures, than the knowledge of things to come; for before the Day wherein the secrets of the heart shall be manifested, ' Almighty [c] God alone doth behold the hidden things,' saith St. Hierome, alleging for proof of this, the text Matt. 6, 4. ' Thy Father That seeth in secret;' Psalm 7, 9. ' God searcheth the hearts and reins;' and 1 Kings 8, 39. ' Thou only knowest the hearts of all the children of men;' but now in the Church of Rome mental prayers are presented to the Saints as well as vocal, and they are believed to receive both the one and the other.

"Secondly, in the former times [d] it was a great question, whether at all, or how far, or after what manner, the spirits of the dead did know the things that concerned us here: and con-

---

[a] Amb. de Sacr. vi. 4.
[b] Quæstt. ad Antioch. ap. Ath. t. 2. p. 303.
[c] Hier. l. 5. in Ezech. c. 16. l. 4. in Ezech. c. 14. l. 4. in Jerem. c. 20. l. 1. in Matt. c. 9. Chrys. in Matt. Hom. 29. Gennad. de Eccl. dogm. c. 81. Cass. Collat. 7. c. 13. Sedul. in Rom. 2. Paschas. de Sp. S. ii. 1 ; et alios passim.
[d] Aug. in Ps. 108. enarr. 1.

sequently, whether they pray for us only ' in* general,' and for the particulars God answereth us according to our several necessities, where, when, and after what manner He pleaseth.   Anselmus Laudunensis, in his interlineal gloss upon that text, ' Abraham is ignorant of us and Israel knoweth us not,' (Is. 63, 16.) noteth that Augustine saith, that ' the dead, even the Saints, do not know what the living do, no not their own sons.'   And indeed St. Augustine in his book of the care for the dead[f], maketh this inference upon that place of Scripture.   ' If such great Patriarchs as these were ignorant, what was done to the people that descended from them, unto whom (believing God) the people itself was promised to come from their stock; how do the dead interpose themselves in knowing and furthering the things and acts of the living?' and afterwards draweth these conclusions from thence, which Hugo[g] de Sancto Victore, borrowing from him, hath inserted into his book De spiritu et anima, cap. 29.   ' The[h] spirits of the dead be there, where they do neither see nor hear the things that are done or fall out to men in this life[i].'   ' Yet have they such a care of the living, although they know not at all what they do, as we have care of the dead, although we know not what they do.'   ' The[j] dead indeed do not know what is done here while it is here in doing: but afterward they may hear it by such as die and go unto them from hence; yet not altogether, but as much as is permitted to the one to tell, fit for the other to hear.   They may know it also by the angels, which be here present with us and carry our souls unto them, they may know also by the revelation of God's Spirit such of the things done here which is necessary for them to know.'—

And then having further shewn that Gratian (Decr. p. 2. caus. 3. qu. 2. c. 29.) holds that the saints do not know what is done here; that P. Lombard holds it not *incredible* that they do, and that " our petitions are made known to them in the Word of God which they contemplate, (l. iv. dist. 45.) that Scotus (ib. q. 4.) and Gab.

---

[f] Aug. de Cur. pro Mort. c. 16.   " That the Saints in general are concerned for the Church, and can pray, and do in fact pray for it, is confessed by Melancthon, (Conf. Aug. art. de Invoc. Sanct.) Brentius, (Conf. Wirtemb. c. de Inv. Sanct.) Chemnitz (Exam. Conc. Trid. c. 3). Calvin also (Inst. 3, 20, 21, and 24) is not opposed to this opinion." Bellar. de Missâ, ii. 8.

[f] c. 13.

[g] Lib. de Sp. et An. t. 3. Op. Aug. qui id. est cum l. 2. de Anim. inter. Op. Hug. Vict.

[h] In de Cur. pro Mort. c. 13. [the book is later than both, containing extracts from both, see Aug. Opp. t. vi. App. p. 39. ed. Ben.   The passages alleged by Abp. Ussher are from a genuine work.]

[i] Ib. c. 14.

[j] Ib. c. 15.

Biel. (in Can. Miss. lect. 21.) hold it" *probable* that God specially reveals to them prayers made to them, he thus contrasts the positiveness of later writers.

Cardinal Bellarmine[k] supposeth, that ' if the Saints should have need thus of a new revelation, the Church would not so boldly say unto all the Saints, ' Pray for us,' but would sometime entreat of God [l], that he would reveal our prayers unto them.' Yet because ' it seemeth unto him superfluous to desire ordinarily of them that they should pray for us, which cannot ordinarily understand what we do in particular, but know only in general that we are exposed to many dangers;' he resolveth, that, ' although[m] there may be some doubt, in what manner the Saints may know things that be absent, and which are sometimes delivered by the affection of the heart alone; yet it is certain that they do know them.' ' And you must note,' says Dr. Pesantius[n], ' that this is to be held for a point of faith, that the Saints do know the prayers, which we pour unto them, *because* otherwise they should be made in vain.' So that to make good the Popish manner of praying unto Saints, that which was at the first but probable and problematical, must now be held to be *de fide* and an undoubted axiom of divinity.

" Thirdly, in the Popish invocation, formal and absolute prayers are tendered to the Saints, but the compellations of them used at first, were commonly either wishes only or requests of the same nature with those which are in this kind usually made unto the living; where the requester is oftentimes superior to him whose prayers he desireth, (which standeth not well with the condition of prayer properly so called,) and they that are requested, be evermore accounted in the number of those that pray for us, but none of those that are prayed unto by us. Of this you may hear, if you please, what one of the more moderate Romanists writeth. ' If[o] it were lawful for the Prophet to call to the Angels and the whole host of Heaven, and to exhort them that they would praise God, which notwithstanding they do continually without any one admonishing them, whereby nothing else but a certain abundance of desire of the amplifying of God's glory is declared : why may it not be lawful also out of a certain abundance of godly desire to call upon those blessed spirits which by the society of the same body are conjoined with us ; and to exhort them, that they should do that, which we believe they otherwise do of themselves ?' That to say, ' All ye

[k] De Eccl. Triumph. l. 1. c. 20.
[l] Id. de Purg. 2. 15.
[m] l. 1. c. 20. ut sup.
[n] In 1. pt. Thom. Quæst. 12. art. 10. Disp. 7. Conc. 6.
[o] G. Cassand. Schol. in Hymn. Eccl. Op. p. 224.

Saints, pray unto God for me;' should import as much, as if it were said, ' Would to God, that all the Saints did pray unto God for me!' ' I wish earnestly that all the Saints should pray to God for me.' Thus writeth Cassander, in his notes upon the ancient ecclesiastical hymns, published by him in the year 1556, who being challenged for this by some others of that side, added this further to give them better satisfaction, ' When [p] I did see that it was not necessary that we should hold that the Saints do understand our prayers; I thought it was sufficient to put back the calumnies of some, if we should say that these interpellations might be expounded by way of wishing or desiring: which hath less absurdity in it, and is agreeable to the examples of the holy Scriptures. But if any man would have such compellations as these to be taken also for an intimation of the desire, and a direct speaking unto them, I do not gainsay it. Notwithstanding I would think that a tacit condition ought to be understood in such an intimation: such as Gregory Nazianzen doth express in the formal oration of his sister Gorgonia when he saith, if thou hast any care at all of our speeches, and holy souls receive this honour from God, that they have notice of such things as these, do thou accept this oration of ours.'

Then, having shewn that even " in the very darkest times of the Papacy" " some famous men" were related to have thought such prayers superfluous, " many" that they were only prayers to God " that the merits of the Saints may help us," not properly to themselves, he adds a

" Fourth difference betwixt the Popish prayers and the interpellations used in the ancient time. For by the doctrine and practice of the Church of Rome, the Saints in Heaven are not only made joint petitioners with us, (as the Saints are upon earth,) but also our attorneys and advocates; who carry the suit for us, not by the pleading of Christ's merits alone, but by bringing in their own merits likewise, upon the consideration of the dignity or condignity whereof it is believed, that God yieldeth to the motions they make unto Him on our behalf. ' We [q] pray unto the Saints (saith the Master of the Sentences) that they may intercede for us, that is to say, that their merits may help us, and that they may will our good; for they willing it, God doth will it, and so it will be effected.' ' We ought to intreat the Apostles and the other Saints (saith Hugo [r] de Prato) in all our necessities; because they are our advocates and the means

---

p Id. Ep. 19. ad Molin. p. 1109.
q Petr. Lombard. Sent. l. 4. Dist. 45. and Jacob. de Vitriac. in Lit. maj.
r Serm. 35.

betwixt us and God, by whom God hath ordained to bestow all
things upon us.' ' Because it is a thing fitting,' (saith Scotus[s],)
' that he that is in bliss should be a coadjutor with God in
procuring the salvation of the elect according to such manner as
this may agree unto him; and to this it is requisite that our
prayers, which are offered unto him, should especially be revealed
unto him, because they lean especially upon the merits of him
as of a mediator bringing us to the salvation which is sought
for; therefore it is probable that God doth specially reveal unto
him that is in bliss such of our prayers as are offered unto him
or unto God in his name.'   But this is an open derogation to
the high prerogative of our Saviour's meritorious intercession,
and a manifest encroachment upon the great office of mediation,
which the most religious and learned among those Fathers, who
desired to be recommended unto the prayers of the Saints, were
so careful to preserve entire unto Him.   ' For what is so proper
to Christ,' saith S. Ambrose[t], ' as to stand by God the Father for
an Advocate of the people?' ' He is the Priest,' saith S. Augustin[u],
' who being now entered within the veil, Alone there of them that
have been partakers of the flesh, doth make intercession for us.'—

" Fifthly, the recommendation of men's selves unto the prayers
of the Saints deceased, which was at first admitted in the
ancient Church, did no way impeach the confidence and boldness
which we have gotten in Christ, to make our immediate approach
to the throne of Grace; which by the invocation of Saints, now
taught in the Church of Rome, is very much impaired.   For to
induce men to the practice of this, the great Majesty of God
and the severity of His justice is propounded unto poor sinners
on the one hand, and the consideration of their own baseness
and unworthiness on the other.   Whereupon it is inferred, that
as well for the manifesting their reverence for God's Majesty,
as the testifying of their submissness and humility, they should
seek to God by the mediation of His Saints; like as men do
seek unto the king by the mediation of his servants.   Which
motives can have no more force to encourage men to the invocation of Saints, than they have to discharge them from the
immediate invocation of God and His Christ.   So among the
causes alleged by Alexander of Hales[x], why we ought to pray
unto the Saints; one is ' in respect of our want in contemplating,
that we who are not able to behold the highest Light in Itself,
may contemplate it in His Saints;' another ' in respect of our
' want in loving: because we miserable men (miserable men
indeed that do so) or some of us, at least, are more affected

[s] In 4. Sent. Dist. 45. Quæst. 4.
[t] In Ps. 39.
[u] In Ps. 64.
[x] Summ. pt. 4. Quæst. 26. memb. 3. art. 5.

sometimes unto some Saint, than unto our Lord Himself; and therefore God, having compassion on our misery, is pleased that we should pray unto His Saints;' and a third 'in respect of the reverence of God; that a sinner who hath offended God, because he dareth not to come unto Him in his own person, may have recourse unto the Saints by imploring their patronage.' The like we read in Gabriel Biel [y], handling the same argument. 'This is a singular consolation (saith he) to sinners, who have oftentimes more mind to the interpellation of the Saints than of the Judge: whose defect of holiness also, other men's goodness is able to supply:' and it maketh [z] 'for the reverence of God, that a sinner who hath offended God, as it were, not daring for the dross of his sin to appear in his proper person, before the most high and dreadful Majesty, should have recourse unto the Saints, who are most pure and grateful to God: who may present the sinner's prayers unto the Most High, and by adjoining their merits and prayers thereunto, might make the same more fit for the audience, more pleasing and more grateful.' Therefore, Salmeron [a], the Jesuit, sticketh not to deliver his opinion plainly; that the praying unto God by the Saints seemeth to him better than the praying unto Him immediately, as for other reasons, ' so because the Church, which hath the Spirit of Christ; (though St. Augustine surely would have judged such a Church to have been led by the spirit of Antichrist rather than of Christ;) ' most frequently hath recourse unto God by the Saints, but cometh more rarely unto God by itself;' and also because the praying of God by the invocation of Saints doth argue greater humility; as may be seen in the Centurion, (Luke 7, 6. 7.)' whereunto he applieth also the saying of David, ' He hath had a respect to the prayer of the humble, and did not despise their prayers [b];' and of Judith, ' The prayer of the humble and meek hath always pleased Thee.'

" Thus in the days of the Apostles themselves, under the pretence of humility [c], some laboured to bring into the Church ' the worshipping of Angels,' which carried with it ' a shew of wisdom,' (as St. Paul speaketh of it,) and such a shew as was not far unlike unto that wherewith our Romish Doctors do cozen simple people nowadays. ' For this' (saith Theodoret [d]) ' did they counsel should be done,' (namely, that men should pray unto Angels,) ' pretending humility, and saying that the God of all things was invisible and inaccessible and incomprehensible,

y In Canon. Miss. Lect. 30.
z Lect. 31.
a In 1 Tim. 2. Disp. 7. sect. ult.
b Ps. 102, 17. Judith 9, 16.
c Coloss. 2, 18. 23.
d In Col. 2.

and that it was fit we should procure God's favour by the means of angels,' whereas St. Chrysostom [e], treating of Christian humility, sheweth that the faithful who are furnished with that grace, do notwithstanding ' ascend beyond the highest tops of heaven, and passing by the Angels present themselves before the regal throne itself.—

"Sixthly, The Romanists repose such confidence in the intercession of the saints, that they look to receive far greater benefit by them, than by their own prayers. Which conceit how distasteful it was to the ancient Doctors, St. Chrysostom [f] may be a sufficient witness, who laboured exceedingly to root out this erroneous opinion, when it first began to shew itself in his time. And therefore he is bold to affirm, not only that we have no such needs of others, that we may entreat by them, but also that God then doth most, when we do not use the entreaties of others.—

" Seventhly and principally it is to be considered, that invocation is attributed to Saints in the Church of Rome as a part of the worship due unto them : yea as eximium adorationis genus, (for so doth Cardinal Bellarmine [g] pronounce it to be,) ' an eminent kind of adoration.' For ' we do not honour the Saints' (saith Azorius [h] the Jesuit) ' with that worship only wherewith we do men that excel in virtue, wisdom, power, or any other dignity, but also with Divine worship and honour which is an act of Religion. For that worship which is given to men of excellency, is an act and office not of Religion, but of another inferior virtue, which is called observance.' And whereas it is as clear as the noonday, that the giving of divine honour and worship unto any creature is flat idolatry, the poor man weeneth that he and his fellows may be excused from being idolaters, because they do not give divine worship and honour unto the Saints for themselves, but for God Who hath made them Saints : as if God, Who cannot endure that His glory should be given unto another, would be mocked with such toys as these. Indeed they were wont heretofore to delude men commonly with an idle distinction of Dulia and Latria [i], but now, ' it [k] is the opinion of the most and the wisest of them, that it is one and the selfsame virtue of Religion which containeth both Latria and Dulia.' Whereas it hath been the constant doctrine of the ancient Church, that all religious worship (whereof prayer by the judgment of all men, as well Heathen as Christian, hath been always esteemed to be an

[e] In Matt. Hom. 65.
[f] In Act. 16. Hom. 36.
[g] Præf. in Controv. de Eccl. Triumph.
[h] Instt. Mor. t. 1. l. ix. c. 10.
[i] They are used as equivalent, Constt. Ap. iii. 7.
[k] Nic. Serarius Litaneut. 2. q. 27. fin.

Q

especial part) is so properly due to God Alone, that without committing of idolatry it cannot be communicated to any creature. For ' in the Catholic Church it is divinely and singularly delivered, that no creature is to be worshipped by the soul, but He only Who is the Creator of all things,' saith St. Augustine[k].   And therefore the ancient Doctors, who thought it not amiss that men should recommend themselves unto the prayers of the Saints departed, held it a thing intolerable notwithstanding, to impart unto any man or angel the worship of invocation.   For to request the help of the prayers of our fellow servants is one thing, and to worship them with the service of invocation is another ; as may be seen in the case of our brethren here on earth, who may not refuse the former without the violation of charity, nor accept the latter at our hands without an open breach of piety.

   " Now that the Fathers judged no otherwise of prayer than hath been said, this may be one good argument ; that when they define it, they do it with express reference to God and no other, as may be seen in those five several definitions thereof which Bellarmine himself repeateth out of them.

   Then, having set these down, and having shewn that the Council of Laodicea anathematized such as invocated Angels[l], and produced sayings from the Fathers to the effect that God only is to be invocated, and " condemning the worship of Angels or any other creature whatsoever," he gives the following sad details from the later ages, and these the more melancholy, since they are not obscure individuals, but men great in their day, who so speak, evidencing how deeply seated these corruptions were in the later Church ;

   ' There[m] wanted not such as would interpret that speech of the Angel unto the holy Virgin, ' Hail, full of grace, the Lord is with thee:' of the equality of her empire with her Son's[n], as if it had been said, ' Even as He, so thou also dost enjoy the same most excellent dignity of ruling.   In[o] the redundance and effusion of grace upon the creatures, the Lord's power and will are so accommodated unto thine, that thou mightest seem to be the first in that both diadem and tribunal.   The Lord is with thee: not so much thou with the Lord, as the Lord is with thee, in that function.'   Then it was taught for good Divinity, that ' from[o] the time wherein the Virgin-mother did conceive in her womb

---

[k] De quant. anim. c. 34. add de mor. Eccl. Cath. c. 30.
[l] The Latin Canonists substituted " angulos" for angelos."
[m] Eman. de Valle de Moura S.T.P. ac Inquisit. Deputatus, Opusc. 1. de Incantat. 1. Ensalmis, s. 1. c. 1. n. 46.
[n] Ib.
[o] Bern. Sen. Serm. 61. art. 1. c. 8.

the Word of God, she hath obtained such a kind of jurisdiction (so to speak) or authority in all the temporal procession of the Holy Ghost, that no creature hath obtained any grace or virtue from God, but according to the dispensation of His holy Mother;" that " because[P] she is the Mother of the Son of God Who doth produce the Holy Ghost, therefore all the gifts, virtues and graces of the Holy Ghost are by her hands administered to whom she pleaseth, how she pleaseth, and as much as she pleaseth." That she[q] hath singularly obtained of God this office from eternity ; as herself doth testify, Prov. viii. 23. ' I was ordained from everlasting,' namely, a dispenser of celestial graces; and that in[r] this respect, Cant. vii. 4. it is said of her, ' Thy neck is a tower of ivory,' because that as by the neck the vital spirits do descend from the head into the body ; so by the Virgin the vital graces are transmitted from Christ the Head into His mystical body, the fulness of grace being in Him, as in the head from whence the influence cometh, and in her as in the neck through which it is transfused unto us ; so that take away the patronage of the Virgin, you stop as it were the sinner's breath that he is not able to live any longer.

" Then men stuck not to teach, that unto her " all[s] power was given in heaven and in earth." So that for " heaven" when our Saviour ascended thither, this might be assigned for one reason (among others) why He left His mother behind Him, " lest[u] perhaps the Court of Heaven might have been in a doubt whom they should rather go to meet, their Lord or their Lady;" and for " earth" she[x] might rightly apply unto herself that in the first of Ezra " all the kingdoms of the earth hath the Lord given unto me." And we may say unto her again that in Tobit xiii. " Thy kingdom endureth for all ages." And in the cxliv. or cxlv. Psalm, " Thy kingdom is a kingdom of all ages." That howsoever she was " the[y] noblest person that was or ever should be in the World, and of so great perfection, that although she had not been the Mother of God, she ought nevertheless to have been the Lady of the world; yet according to the laws whereby the world is governed, by the right of inheritance she did deserve the principality and king-

[P] Id. ib.
[q] Id. ib. art. 3. c. 3.
[r] Id. ib. art. 1. c. 8. art. 2. c. 10. ex Pseudo-Hieron. Serm. de Assumpt. Mariæ. Jo. Herolt. in Serm. Discip. de Temp. Serm. 163. Blas. Viegas in Apoc. c. 12. Comm. 2. s. 10. n. 1. 2.
[s] Viegas, ib. s. 2. n. 6.
[t] P. Damian. Serm. 1. de Nat. B. Mariæ. t. 5. Surii Sept. 8.
[u] Anselm de Excell. B. Virg. c. 7. and following him, Bern. de Bust. in Mariali, p. 11. Serm. 1. p. 3. and Seb. Barrad. Jesuit. Conc. Evang. vi. 11.
[x] Bern. de Bust. l. c. pt. 12. Serm. 1. pt. 1.
[y] Bern. Sen. Serm. 61. art. 1. c. 7.

dom of this world." That " Christ[m] never made any legacy of His Monarchy : because that could not be done without the prejudice of His Mother ; and He knew besides that the Mother could make void the Testament of the Son, if it were made unto her prejudice. And therefore that by all this it appeareth most evidently, that Mary the Mother of Jesus by right of inheritance hath the regal dominion over all that be under God." That " as[n] many creatures do serve the glorious Virgin Mary, as serve the Trinity. Namely, all creatures, whatsoever degree they hold among the things created (whether they be spiritual as angels, or rational as men, or corporal as the heavenly bodies or the elements) and all things that are in heaven or in earth, whether they be the damned or the blessed ; all which being brought under the government of God, are subject likewise unto the glorious Virgin, forasmuch as He Who is the Son of God and of the blessed Virgin, being willing as it were to equal in some sort His Mother's sovereignty unto the sovereignty of His Father, even He Who was God did serve His Mother upon earth. Whence Luke ii. 51. it is written of the Virgin and glorious Joseph : ' He was subject unto them,' that as the proposition is true, All things are subject to God's command, even the Virgin herself: so this again is true also, All things are subject to the command of the Virgin, even God Himself." That " considering[o] the blessed Virgin is the Mother of God and God is her Son, and every son is naturally inferior to his mother, and subject unto her, and the mother hath preeminence and is superior to her son ; it therefore followeth that the blessed Virgin is superior to God, and God Himself is subject unto her in respect of the Manhood which He assumed from her," that " howsoever[p] she be subject unto God inasmuch as she is a creature : yet is she said to be superior and preferred before Him, inasmuch as she is His Mother."

" Then men were put in mind that " by[q] sinning after Baptism they seemed to contemn and despise the Passion of Christ : and so that no sinner doth deserve that Christ should any more make intercession for him to the Father : without whose intercession none can be delivered either from the eternal punishment or the temporal, nor from the fault which he hath voluntarily committed. And therefore that it was necessary that Christ should constitute His well-beloved Mother a Mediatrix betwixt us and Him," " and[r] so in this our pilgrimage there is no other

[m] Id. ib.
[n] Id. ib. c. 6.
[o] Bern. de Bust. Marial. p. 9. Serm. 2.
[p] Id. p. 2. Serm. 2.
[q] Jac. de Valent. Episc. Christopol. in expos. Cant. V. Mariæ Magnificat.
[r] Id. ib.

refuge left unto us in our tribulations and adversities but to have recourse unto the Virgin Mary our Mediatrix; that she would appease the wrath of her Son." That " as [s] He is ascended into heaven to appear in the sight of God for men ; (Heb. ix. 24.) so she ought to ascend thither to appear in the sight of her Son for sinners; that so mankind might have always before the face of God, a help like unto Christ for the procuring of his salvation." That " this [t] Empress is of so great authority in the palace of Heaven, that it is lawful to appeal unto her from any grievance, all other intermedial Saints omitted."—" That [u] she is a Chancellor in the court of heaven, and giveth letters of mercy only in this present life ; but for the souls that depart from hence, unto some letters of pure grace, unto others of simple justice, and unto some mixed of justice and grace. For some (say they) were much devoted unto her : and unto them she giveth letters of pure grace, whereby she commandeth glory to be given them, without any pain of Purgatory. Others were miserable sinners and not devoted to her; and unto them she giveth letters of simple justice, whereby she commandeth that condign punishment be taken of them. Others were lukewarm and remiss in devotion ; and to them she giveth letters of justice and grace together: whereby she commandeth that both favour be done unto them, and yet some pain of Purgatory be inflicted upon them for their negligence and sluggishness." And these things they say " are signified in Queen Esther; who wrote letters that the Jews should be saved, and the enemies should be killed, and to the poor small gifts should be given." Yea further also, where [x] King Ahasuerus did proffer unto the said Esther even the half of his kingdom, (Esther v. 3.) thereby (they say) was signified that God bestowed half of His Kingdom upon the blessed Virgin. " That having justice and mercy as the chiefest goods of His Kingdom, He retained Justice unto Himself, and granted Mercy unto her:" and " therefore [y] that if a man do find himself aggrieved in the Court of God's Justice, he may appeal to the Court of Mercy of His Mother," she being that ' throne of grace' whereof the Apostle speaketh (Heb. iv. 16.), ' Let us go boldly unto the throne [z] of Grace, that we may receive Mercy, and find Grace to help in time of need.' They tell us that [a] it is for the ornament of an earthly Kingdom, that

---

[s] Bern. de Bust. Marial. p. 11. Serm. 2. memb. 1.
[t] Id. p. 3. Serm. 3. in Excell. 4.
[u] Id. p. 12. Serm. 2. memb. 1. in. Excell. 22.
[x] Gabr. Biel. in Can. Missæ. lect. 80. vid. Joh. Gerson. tract 4. sup. Magnificat.
[y] Bern. de Bust. Marial. p. 3. Serm. 3. in Excell. 4.
[z] Id. ib. Exc. 5. and p. 5. Serm. 7. in fin.
[a] Id. p. 9. Serm. 2.

it should have both a King and a Queen, and therefore when any king hath not a wife, his subjects often do request him to take one.   Hereupon they say, that the eternal King and omnipotent Emperor, minding to adorn the kingdom of Heaven above, did frame this blessed Virgin, to the end He might make her the lady and Empress of His kingdom and empire; that the prophecy of David might be verified, saying unto her in the Psalm: ' Upon Thy right hand did stand the Queen in clothing of gold.'   That " she[b] is an Empress because she is the spouse of the eternal Emperor: of Whom it is said, (John iii. 29.) He that hath the Bride is the Bridegroom, and that when God did deliver unto her the empire of the world and all the things contained therein, He said unto her that which we read in the first of the Æneids :

> His ego nec metas rerum nec tempora pono ;
> Imperium sine fine dedi.

" That she is " the Empress[c] also of heaven and earth, because she did bear the heavenly Emperor; and therefore that she can ask of Him what she will, and obtain it.   That this was figured in the history of the Kings, where the mother of Solomon said unto him : ' I desire one petition of thee, do not confound my face:' for then should He confound her face if He did deny that which she requested;" and that " if in respect of her maternal jurisdiction she hath command of her Son Who was subject unto her : (as we read, Luke ii. 51.) then much more hath she command over all the creatures that are subject to her Son." That " this[d] mighty God did (as far as He might) make His Mother partner of His Divine Majesty and power ; giving unto her of old the sovereignty both of celestial things and mortal; ordering at her pleasure (as the patronage of men did require) the earth, the seas ; Heaven and Nature ; at her liking, and by her, bestowing on mortal men His Divine treasures and heavenly gifts.   So as all might understand that whatsoever doth flow into the earth from that eternal and glorious fountain of good things, doth flow by Mary."   That " she[e] is constituted over every creature ; and whosoever boweth his knee unto Jesus, doth fall down also and supplicate unto His Mother ; so that the glory of the Son may be judged, not so much to be common with the Mother as to be the very same."   That

---

[b] Id. P. 3. Serm. 3. Excell. 4.
[c] Id. Ib.
[d] Horat. Turselin. Jesuit. and in Ep. Dedic. Hist. Lauret. ad Card. Aldobrandinum.
[e] Arnold. Carnot. Tract. de Laud. Virg.

" so ʳ great is her glory that she exceedeth the nature of Angels and men joined together, as far in glory, as the circumference of the firmament exceedeth his centre in magnitude, when she understandeth herself in her Son to be, as His other self, clothed with the Deity." That she being " the Mother ᵍ of God doth assume unto herself of the omnipotency of her Son (upon which she leaneth) as much as she pleaseth." And that she " doth ʰ come before the golden altar of human reconciliation not intreating only but commanding ; a Mistress, not a Maid." They tell us that the blessed Virgin herself appeared once unto Thomas Becket and used this speech unto him, " Rejoice ᶦ and be glad and be joyful with me : because my glory doth excel the dignity and joy of all the Saints and all the blessed spirits ; and I alone have greater glory than all the Angels and Saints together. Rejoice, because that as the Sun doth enlighten the day and the world, so my brightness doth enlighten the whole celestial world. Rejoice, because the whole host of Heaven obeyeth me, revereneeth and honoureth me. Rejoice, because my Son is always obedient unto me and my will, and all my prayers He always heareth." (Or as others ᵏ do relate it, " The will of the Blessed Trinity and mine is one and the same; and whatsoever doth please me the whole Trinity with unspeakable favour doth give consent unto.") " Rejoice, because God doth always at my pleasure reward my servitors in this world, and in the world to come. Rejoice, because I sit next to the holy Trinity, and am clothed with my body glorified. Rejoice, because I am certain and sure that these my joys shall always stand, and never be finished or fail. And whosoever by rejoicing with these spiritual joys shall worship me in this world, at the time of the departure of his soul out of the body, he shall obtain my presence; and I will deliver his soul from the malignant enemies, and present it in the sight of my Son, that it may possess joys with me." They tell us that " many (many whores ᶦ for example, that would not sin on Saturday for the reverence of the Virgin, whatsoever they did on the Lord's day) seem to have the blessed Virgin in greater veneration than Christ her Son ; moved thereunto out of simplicity more than out of knowledge. Yet that the Son of God doth bear with the simplicity of these men and women, because He is not ignorant that the honour of the Mother doth redound to the Child." (Prov. xvii. 6.) They argue further that " if ᵐ a Cardinal have this

ᶠ Bern. de Bust. Marial. P. 12. Serm. 2. Excell. 21.
ᵍ Id. P. 12. Serm. 2. Excell. 28.
ʰ P. Damian. Serm. 1. de Nat. B. Mariæ.
ᶦ Bern. de Bust. Marial. P. 20. Serm. 2. sect. ult.
ᵏ Promptuar. Discipuli de Miraculis B. Mariæ, Exempl. 14. p. 8. ed. Mogunt. 1612.
ᶦ Bern. de Bust. P. 6. Serm. 2. Memb. 3.
ᵐ Id. P. 12. Serm. 1. Memb. 3.

privilege, that if he put his cap upon the head of one that is led unto justice, he is freed thereby : then by an argument drawn from the stronger, the cloak of the blessed Virgin is able to deliver us from all evil, her mercy being so large, that if she should see any man who did devoutly make her crown (that is to say, repeat the rosary or chaplet of prayers made for her worship) to be drawn unto punishment in the midst of a thousand devils ; she would presently rescue him, and not permit that any one should have an evil end, who did study reverently to make her crown." They add moreover, that " for[i] every of these crowns a man shall obtain 273758 days of indulgence: and that Pope Sixtus the Fourth granted an indulgence of 12,000 years for every time that a man in the state of grace should repeat this short orizon or salutation of the Virgin, which by many is inserted into her crowns ' Hail, most holy Mary, the mother of God, the queen of Heaven, the gate of Paradise, the Lady of the world. Thou art a singular and pure Virgin: thou didst conceive Christ without sin : thou didst bear the Creator and Saviour of the world, in Whom I do not doubt. Deliver me from all evil, and pray for my sins. Amen.'" In the crowns composed by Bonaventure, this is one of the orizons that is prescribed to be said, ' O[k] Empress, and our most kind Lady, by the authority of a mother command thy most beloved Son, our Lord Jesus Christ, that He would vouchsafe to lift up our minds from the love of earthly unto heavenly desires;' which is suitable to that versicle, which we read in the 35th Psalm of this Lady's Psalter; ' Incline[l] the countenance of God upon us, compel Him to have mercy upon sinners,' the harshness whereof our Romanists have a little qualified in some of their editions, reading thus, " Incline[m] the countenance of thy Son upon us, compel Him by thy prayers to have mercy upon us sinners." The Psalms of this Psalter do all of them begin as David's do, but with this main difference, that where the Prophet in the one aimeth at the advancement of the honour of our Lord, the Friar in the other applieth all to the magnifying of the power and goodness of our Lady. So in the first Psalm: Blessed is the man (quoth Bonaventure) that loveth thy name, O Virgin Mary, thy grace shall comfort his soul ; and in the others following; Lady[n], how are they multiplied that trouble me ? with thy tempest shalt thou persecute and scatter them. Lady[o], suffer me not to be rebuked in the fury of God, nor to be judged in His wrath. My Lady[p], in thee have I put my trust: deliver me from my enemies,

---

[i] Ib.   [k] Bonaventura Corona B. M. V. Opp. t. 6. Romæ, 1588.
[l] Psalt. B. M. V. 26.   [m] Psalt. Bonaventuræ seorsim editæ. Paris. 1596, in Capeleto Dominicæ 2.   [n] Ps. 3.   [o] Ps. 6.   [p] Ps. 7.

O Lady. In our Lady[p] put I my trust; for the sweetness of the mercy of her name. How[q] long wilt thou forget me, O Lady, and not deliver me in the day of tribulation? Preserve[r] me, O Lady, for in thee have I put my trust: and impart unto me the drops of thy grace. I[s] will love thee, O Lady of heaven and earth, and I will call upon thy name among the nations. 'The heavens[t] declare thy glory: and the fragrance of thine ointments is spread among the nations.' Hear[u] us, Lady, in the day of trouble; and turn thy merciful face unto our prayers. Unto thee[x], O Lady, have I lifted up my soul: in the judgment of God, by thy prayers, I shall not be ashamed. Judge me[y], Lady, for I have departed from my innocency, but because I will trust in thee, I shall not be weakened. In thee[z], O Lady, have I put my trust, let me never be confounded: in thy favour receive me. Blessed[a] are they whose hearts do love thee, O Virgin Mary; their sins by thee shall mercifully be washed away. Lady[b], judge those that hurt me: and rise up against them and plead my cause. Waiting[c] have I waited for thy grace; and thou hast done unto me according to the multitude of the mercy of thy name. Lady[d], thou art our refuge in all our necessities; and the powerful strength treading down the enemy. Have mercy[e] upon me, O Lady, who art called the mother of mercy, and according to the bowels of thy mercies, cleanse me from all mine iniquities. Save me[f], Lady, by thy name and deliver me from mine unrighteousness. Have mercy[g] upon me, O Lady, have mercy upon me: because my heart is prepared to search out thy will, and in the shadow of thy wings will I rest. Let[h] Mary arise; and let her enemies be scattered: let them all be trodden down under her feet. In thee[i], O Lady, have I put my trust, let me never be put to confusion: deliver me in thy mercy, and cause me to escape. Give[k] the King thy judgment, O God, and thy mercy to the Queen His Mother. Lady[l], the Gentiles are come into the inheritance of God, whom thou by thy merits hast confederated unto Christ. Thy mercies[m], O Lady, will I sing for ever. God[n] is the Lord of revenges, but thou the mother of mercy dost bow Him to take pity. O come[o] let us sing unto our Lady; let us make a joyful noise to Mary, our Queen, that brings salvation. O sing[p] unto our Lady a new song, for she hath done marvellous things. O[q] give thanks unto the Lord, for He is good: give thanks unto His Mother, for her mercy endureth for ever. Lady[r], despise not my praise: and vouchsafe to accept

[p] Ps. 10.	[q] Ps. 13.	[r] Ps. 16.	[s] Ps. 18.	[t] Ps. 19.
[u] Ps. 20.	[x] Ps. 25.	[y] Ps. 26.	[z] Ps. 31.	[a] Ps. 32.
[b] Ps. 35.	[c] Ps. 40.	[d] Ps. 46.	[e] Ps. 51.	[f] Ps. 54.
[g] Ps. 57.	[h] Ps. 68.	[i] Ps. 71.	[k] Ps. 72.	[l] Ps. 79.
[m] Ps. 89.	[n] Ps. 94.	[o] Ps. 95.	[p] Ps. 98.	[q] Ps. 107 and 118.
[r] Ps. 109.				

this Psalter which is dedicated unto thee. The [a] Lord said unto our Lady, Sit thou, My mother, at My right hand. They [f] that trust in thee, O mother of God, shall not fear from the face of the enemy. Except [u] our Lady build the house of our heart, the building thereof will not continue. Blessed [x] are all they who fear our Lady, and blessed are all they who know to do thy will and thy good pleasure. Out [y] of the deep have I cried unto thee, O Lady : Lady, hear my voice. Lady [z], remember David, and all that call upon thy name. O [a] give thanks unto the Lord, because He is good : because by His most sweet Mother the Virgin Mary is His mercy given. Blessed be thou [b], O Lady, which teachest thy servants to war, and strengthenest them against the enemy. And so the last Psalm is begun with, Praise our Lady in her Saints, praise her in her virtues and miracles ; and ended accordingly, with, Omnis spiritus laudet Dominam nostram ; Let every spirit (or every thing that hath breath) praise our Lady.'

To this we may adjoin the Psalter [c] of the salutations of the Virgin, framed by John Peckham, Archbishop of Canterbury, which is not yet printed. His preface he beginneth thus : ' I purpose to write the praises of the Holy Virgin ; who delivers us from prison through her Son, quickening our whole race by a work wondrous in efficacy :' and endeth with a prayer to the Blessed Virgin, ' that she would release the sins of all those for whom he prayed, and cause both his own name and theirs to be written in the book of life.' Then followeth his first Psalm : wherein he prayeth, that ' she would make us to meditate often God's law,' and, afterwards ' to be made blessed in the glory of God's kingdom.' His other 149 Psalms (which are fraught with the same kind of stuff) I pass over. But Bernardinus de Senis [d], his boldness may not be forgotten ; who thinketh that " God will give him leave to maintain, that the Virgin Mary did more unto Him, or at least as much, as He Himself did unto all mankind, and that we may say for our comfort, (forsooth) that in respect of the blessed Virgin (whom God Himself did make notwithstanding), God after a sort is more bound unto us, than we are unto Him." With which absurd and wretched speculation, Bernardinus de Busti [e] after him was so well pleased, that he dareth to revive again this odious comparison.—" But O most grateful Virgin, didst not thou something to God. Didst not thou make Him any recompence? Truly, (if it be lawful to speak it) thou in some respect didst

---

[a] Ps. 110. [t] Ps. 125. [u] Ps. 127. [x] Ps. 128. [y] Ps. 130.
[z] Ps. 132. [a] Ps. 136. [b] Ps. 144.
[c] Called by J. Pits, de Ill. Angl. Script. p. 380. Psalter. Medit. B. Mariæ.
[d] Serm. 61. art. 1. c. 11.
[e] Marial, p. 6. Serm. 2. memb. 3.

greater things to God, than God Himself did to thee and to all
mankind. I will therefore speak that, which thou out of thy
humility hast past in silence. For thou only didst sing, ' He
that is mighty hath done to me great things,' but I do sing and
say, that ' thou hast done greater things to Him that is mighty.' "
Neither is that vision much better, which the same author f
reciteth as shewed to St. Francis, or (as others g would have it)
to his companion Friar Lion; touching the two ladders that
reached from earth to heaven ; the one red, upon which Christ
leaned, from whence many fell backward and could not ascend;
the other white, upon which the holy Virgin leaned : the help
whereof such as used, were by her received with a cheerful
countenance, and so with facility ascended into Heaven.
Neither yet that sentence, which came first from Anselm h, and
was after him used by Ludolphus Saxo i the Carthusian, and
Chrysostomus à Visitatione k the Cistercian Monk : that " more
present relief is sometimes found by commemorating the name
of Mary, than by calling upon the Name of our Lord Jesus her
only Son." Which one of our Jesuits l is so far from being
ashamed to defend, that he dareth to extend it further to the
mediation of other Saints also ; telling us very peremptorily, that
" as our Lord Jesus worketh greater miracles by His Saints than
by Himself (John xiv. 12.) so, often He sheweth the force of their
intercession more than of His own."

All which I do lay down thus largely m, not because I take any
delight in rehearsing those things, which deserve rather to be

f Ib. p. 9. Serm. 2. assim. 2.
g Spec. vit. Fransisci et socior. ej. p. 2. c. 45. Spec. exempl. dist. 7.
exempl. 41.
h de Excell. B. Virg. c. 6.
i de Vita Christi, p. 2. c. 60.
k de Verb. Dominæ, t. 2. l. 2. c. 2.
l H. Fitz-Simon of the Mass, l. 2. p. 2. c. 3.
m Melancholy as all this, it is only a specimen of what might be produced;
thus Whitaker (adv. Camp. Rat. 9. p. 44.) quotes from the Prosa Missæ de
Concept. " Thou art the sure hope of the miserable, truly the mother of the
parentless, thou art the relief of the oppressed, the medicine of the weak, *thou
art all things to all;*" and from a book of " hours" entitled the Hist. sec.
chorum August. de Comm. Beatiss. Virg. Mariæ (Opp. p. 219.) framed,
(which is the more shocking) on the Magnificat, which it corrects, " Rejoice,
heavenly Lady, exalt and magnify God thy Saviour, Who made thee alone of
thy kind ; thou willedst to call thyself the ' handmaiden' of Jesus Christ, but
as the Divine law teaches, thou art Mistress over Him (tu ipsius es Domina)
for right and reason have it, that the mother should be set over (præesse) the
son ; therefore pray suppliantly and direct with authority (præcipe sublimiter)
that in the eventide of the world He lead us to the kingdoms above ;" and
" Thou alone peerless whom the Lord chose to be mediatrix between God and
man, &c." and in " the Office to her, reformed by Pius V." " Mary mother of
grace, mother of mercy, do thou protect us from the enemy, and receive us at
the hour of death."

buried in everlasting oblivion ; but first, that the world may take notice, what kind of monster is nourished in the Papacy under that strange name of Hyperdulia : the bare discovery whereof, I am persuaded, will prevail as much with a mind that is touched with any zeal of God's honour, as all other arguments and authorities whatsoever. Secondly, that such unstable souls as look back upon Sodom and have a lust to return unto Egypt again, may be advised to look a little into this sink, and consider with themselves, whether the steam that ariseth from thence be not so noisome, that it is not to be endured by one that hath any sense left in him of piety. And thirdly, that such as be established in the present truth, may be thankful to God for this great mercy vouchsafed unto them.

POSTSCRIPT.

SINCE the above has been in type, I have been furnished with a melancholy confirmation of the truth of Mr. Newman's words, that the " received doctrine of the Roman schools of that day" is " unhappily that of this day too;" that

" The present authoritative teaching of the Church of Rome, to judge by what we see of it in public, goes very far indeed to substitute another Gospel for the true one. Instead of setting before the soul the Holy Trinity—it does seem to me as a popular system to preach the Blessed Virgin and the Saints."

It would probably be a first impression on reading these extracts from Abp. Ussher, that he had with much learning brought together a mass of objectionable language, which it might be hoped was now done away ; that all these were the exaggerations of individual minds, and that it was not fair to charge them as teaching now received in the Roman Church. This was my own hope ; I reprinted them in illustration of the meaning of the Article, but certainly, little thinking of imputing them to Rome at the present day. The contrary, however, of all this is sadly the case. The same extracts which Abp. Ussher adduces as illustrating the difference between " the Romish doctrine of the invocation of Saints" and ancient addresses to them, are, in " the Glories of Mary Mother of God by Saint Alphonsus Liguori, and carefully revised by a Catholic Priest," (third ed. Dublin, 1837,) adduced as authoritative teaching. The subjects of the early chapters, which they are adduced to establish, are " how great should be our confidence in Mary, Queen of Mercy," (§. 1.) " as our Mother," (§. 2.) " the great love borne us by Mary, our Mother," (§. 3.) that " Mary is *the* refuge of repentant sinners" and so (§. 4.) " our life, since she obtains us the pardon of our sins," (c 2. §. 1.) " because she obtains us perseverance," (§. 2.) " the *necessity* of Mary's intercession in order to obtain salvation," (c. 5.) &c. The sayings of Bernardine of Sienna, Albertus M., Bonaventure, &c. are alleged as authorities. It is still alleged as a true saying, " All is subject to Mary's empire, even God," (p. 138, see Abp. Ussher, above p. 196.) It is not, of course, to be supposed that no mention should be made of her Son, or from time to time that her intercession is available through her Son, or that " Jesus is our Redeemer, Mary our Advocate." (p. 88.) " Jesus is my only hope, and after Him you, O Virgin Mary " (p. 90.) One could not imagine any thing written by a Christian in entire forgetfulness of his Lord ; but these are but scanty; the main object of the work is, (as it professes,) " the Glories of Mary," and these are so set forth, as for the most part to end in her, to place her where a Catholic would expect mention of his Lord. Thus at the hour of death, it is said, " May I invoke you during life, and die when calling on—Mary, my Mother, my blessed amiable Mother." (p. 88.) To whom again could it be thought that such language as the following is addressed ?

" If you grant me your aid, what can I fear ? during life and at my death, your name and remembrance shall be the delight of my soul, p. 74. I desire to consecrate myself more particularly to your service—dispose of me according to your good pleasure ; direct me ; I abandon myself wholly to your conduct ; never more let me be guided by myself; chastise me, if I disobey you ; your correction will be sweet and agreeable. (Ps. cxli. 5.) I am then no longer mine, *I am all yours.*" (p. 50.) " My sins render me unworthy of approaching you. I should expect nothing but chastisement from your hands.— I place in you *all my confidence,* and provided I may be happy enough to die before your image, I shall firmly hope to join in heaven that innumerable multitude who have been saved by

your intercession." (p. 53, 4.)   " How dare a sinner, unworthy
as I, appear before you?   I am the last of sinners; I have
offended the Divine Majesty more than any other; since I cannot recall the past, help me to amend the present." (p. 57.)
" O consolation of the afflicted! have pity upon me; remorse
of conscience gnaws me; my best actions are but imperfectly
performed; hell awaits to carry off my soul; divine Justice
must be satisfied; what then shall become of me?   what shall
be my eternal lot?" (p. 83.)   " He who is protected by you
cannot be lost; heaven and earth confess it.   Hence though
all creatures forget me, though the whole world abandon me,
provided you forsake me not, I should think myself secure." (p.
90.)   " I cannot abandon myself to despair; because you are
my refuge, and your clemency is unbounded." (p. 135.)   " All
power has been given unto you in heaven and on earth;
nothing is impossible to you, for you can give hope to the de-
sponding." (p. 138.)

Again, it is, of course, presupposed and sometimes expressed that S. Mary is a mediatrix with our Lord, that
her power is derived from Him, and through Him; but
then, at best, it is a power absolutely vested in her; it is
not the Intercession of a creature, however exalted; it is
the will of one, whose will is complied with and obeyed.
She stands between the soul and its Judge; it need not
go to its Judge; it has but to gain the intercession of His
Mother, and leave the rest to her.

" Because she opens at pleasure the abyss of the Divine
mercy, no sinner, however enormous his crimes may be, can
perish if he is protected by Mary." (p. 25.)   " Every petition
she offers is as a law emanating from the Lord, by which He
obliges Himself to be merciful to those for whom she inter-
cedes." (p. 24.)   " You have the keys of the Divine mercy, draw
on this inexhaustible treasure, and dispense its riches to this
poor sinner, in proportion to his immense wants." (p. 136.)
" When Mary," says S. Peter Damian, " presents herself
before Jesus, the altar of reconciliation, she rather seems to
dictate than to supplicate, and has more the air of a Queen
than a subject"—" the saint (Bernardine) wishes to insinuate
that God hears Mary's prayers, as if they were commands."
' The Lord, O Mary, has so exalted you,' says S. Anselm,
' that His favour has rendered you omnipotent.'   ' Yes,' says
Richard of S. Laurence, ' Mary is omnipotent, for according to
all laws the queen enjoys the same privileges as the king, and
that power may be equal between the Son and the Mother.' "
(p. 138.)   " Albertus M. makes you say, ' It suffices to
entreat me to desire a thing, for whatsoever I wish is neces-

sarily accomplished.'" (p. 139.) "All good comes to us with Mary; he who has found her, has found all grace, all virtue, since there is no good, which he does not obtain through her intercession. She herself warns us that she has *at her disposal all the treasures of the Divinity.* ' With me are glory and riches, that I may enrich them that love me.' Hence S. Bonaventure wishes us ever to keep our eyes on the hands of Mary, to receive from them all that is necessary for our true welfare." (comp. Ps. 123, 2.) p. 88. "Another time, our Blessed Lord said to Mary in the presence of St Gertrude, ' I know that in virtue of My Omnipotence I have invested you with power to deal out mercy in such a measure as you find good, to all sinners who invoke you.'" (p. 104, 5.) "We, holy Virgin, hope for grace and salvation from you, and since you need but say the word, ah, do so, you shall be heard, and we shall be saved." (p. 144.)

To add one more definite statement from a popular and authoritative work, the " Treatise on the Scapular," (c. 7. p. 43.)

" It is a Catholic proposition, that the most sacred Virgin Mary, by a *participated* authority, granted to her as Mother of Jesus Christ, can do much in all things, where mercy doth contend with justice. Wherefore S. Anselm saith, "There is no doubt but the Blessed Virgin Mary, by maternal right, is with Christ president of heaven and earth. S. John Damascene saith, It is fitting and convenient that Mary should possess what is her Son's.—Hence we may infer how the Blessed Virgin can free the souls of her devouts out of purgatory, and fulfil her other promises made to the brothers and sisters of the holy Confraternity; to wit, by a power communicated to her by her Son. For she being really Mother of the Word Incarnate, there is in all propriety due to her a certain power, or, as others say, a dominion over all things, as well spiritual as temporal, to which the authority of her Son doth extend itself. So that she hath by a natural right of maternity, a power almost like that of her Son, of which she may serve herself, as often as she shall think good. Relying therefore on this *her participated omnipotency*, and on the efficaciousness of her merits and intercessions, she promised the devouts of her holy habit to free them from the temporary pains of purgatory fire, from the eternal pains of hell-fire, and from many dangers and calamities of this life, as well spiritual as temporal.'

Yet this has been said yet more strongly in " the Glories

of Mary," that she not only "partakes His Omnipotence," but that He has "resigned" it to her.

"Now the King of heaven, Whose bounty is infinite, desiring nothing so ardently as to confer His favours on us, in order to increase our confidence in Him, has given us His Mother for our Mother, and in her hands resigned, (if we might say so,) His omnipotence in the sphere of grace, that we might place in her the hope of our salvation, and all the help necessary to attain it." (p. 85.)

And this power they are fond of representing as belonging to her, not as the creature of whom our Lord deigned to take our nature, but (as before in Abp. Ussher, p. 195. 196. 198. 199. 202.) derived from her own merit towards her Son, as the result of a debt which He owed her. They are painfully fond of placing her in the same relation as The Father.

"Mary owes her Son an infinite gratitude for choosing her for His Mother, but it is not less true to say that Jesus Christ has contracted a species of obligation towards her for the human existence He received from her, and in recompense for this benefit, He honours her by hearing her prayers." (ib. p. 26, 7.)
"Mary has not spared her own Son, her own soul, for the salvation of many." p. 32. "If to evince the love of God the Father for man it is said, that 'He delivered up His own Son for them;' may we not use the same terms, to express the love of Mary? 'Yes,' says S. Bonaventure, 'Mary has so loved us, that she has given us her only Son.' 'She gave Him us,' says F. Nieremberg, 'when in virtue of her jurisdiction over Him as mother, she permitted Him to deliver Himself up to the Jews.' 'She gave Him for us—she hath given this Well-Beloved Son; she sacrificed for us a Son, Who was infinitely dearer to her than herself.' 'If our salvation was then so near her heart.' (p. 41—43.) 'This Divine Saviour Whom she has given to the world.' (p 131.) 'Richard of S. Laurence beautifully explains this passage, (Prov. xxx. 11.) in reference to the holy Virgin, 'The heart of the man of God who trusts in Mary, he shall not want spoils,' for she has snatched from hell its prey, to enrich with spoils our Lord Jesus Christ."
"In taking flesh in your chaste womb, a God has been pleased to become your debtor, in order to place afterwards at your disposal all the treasures of His unbounded mercy." (p. 144.) "as it was revealed to S. Bridget, Jesus has obliged Himself to grant all the desires and requests of His blessed Mother, not willing to

refuse her any thing in heaven, since she has refused Him nothing on earth." (p. 138, 9.)

" S. Germanus says to Mary, ' You, O holy Virgin, have over God the authority of a Mother, and hence you obtain pardon for the most obdurate sinners.'"

So that at last it seems nothing strange, that she should be introduced as upbraiding an apostate, " Thou hast renounced *me* and my Son," (p. 135.) or that she should be addressed by a penitent, " I have by my impurity sinned against God and against *thee*," (p. 80.) or with the attribute of Divinity, " O sweet in *communicating** thyself to those that love you, to those that seek you." (p. 193.)

It is, of course, believed in the abstract, that our Lord is the One Mediator with the Father, and the blessed Virgin a mediatrix only with our Lord; Rome is not charged with denying, but with overlaying the Faith by her additions; but practically, at the best, where is the inducement held out to a sinner to go further than the blessed Virgin, when it is taught that she has all power given her, that she obtains what she wills, that persons need only pray to her? Certainly it is said that none can be saved who do not pray to her, but it is not taught (but the contrary) that those will not be saved who pray to none besides her, who never pray to God. Nor can this be paralleled with the Catholic doctrine of prayer to the Father through the Son; undoubtedly, there may be a form of unconscious Unitarianism lurking under exclusive prayer to our Lord; (as it would also be un-Scriptural and un-Catholic;) but, at least, in such prayers, prayer is offered to Him Who with the Father and the Holy Ghost is One God; in these prayers to the Virgin, the creature is substituted for the Creator as the object of prayer.

Such, it is much to be feared, must be the effect of this teaching on common minds; but, at the very best, her office, as thus set forth, practically takes the place of that which our Blessed Lord deigns to bear. The feelings of

---

* It seems but a following out of this teaching that a heresy is said to exist among the lower ranks in Rome, that in the Holy Eucharist, not only our Lord but His Mother is present. Such a heresy would, again, naturally follow from such teaching as, " Mary and Jesus having but one and the same Flesh, says S. Arnand Abbot, why should not the Mother enjoy, conjointly with the Son, the honours of royalty ?" The application to the Holy Eucharist seems to lie nearer, and were not more profane, than that actually made.

devout affection, trust, and hope amid our sins, "boldness in approaching to the throne of grace," consciousness that we have One Who can have a feeling for our infirmities, which, in the Catholic system, are directed towards our Lord, as being man although God, in the Romanist are turned aside to His Mother. Our Lord is contemplated as God and our Judge, the blessed Virgin has that office which, in the Catholic system, is occupied by the glorified Humanity of our Lord; justice and mercy are no longer met together, but justice is apportioned to our Lord, His other attribute of mercy is divided from Him and given to His Mother. The soul is invited, not to lift itself up to Him, but to rest in His Mother, as finding in her the very attributes, which Holy Scripture and the Catholic Church set forth to us in our Lord.

Some painful evidence of this has been already given by Abp. Ussher; these statements are repeated, and enforced to this day:

" Mary is Queen of mercy alone; she is a sovereign, not to punish sinners but to pardon and forgive them.—Gerson observes that as the kingdom of God consists in mercy and justice, the Lord has, as it were, divided it; reserving to Himself the dominion of justice, and yielding to His Mother that of mercy. S. Thomas confirms this, when he says, that one half of the kingdom of God was given to Mary, when she conceived and brought forth the Eternal Word, so that she became Queen of mercy as her Son is King of justice. A learned interpreter, writing on Ps. lxxii. 1. says to God, ' Lord, you have given justice to the King your Son, because you have reserved mercy for the Queen His Mother.' S. Bonaventure and Ernest Abp of Prague, explain the words in nearly the same terms," (p. 23 ;) " Let us go then, Christians, let us go to this most gracious Queen, and crowd around her throne, (comp. Heb. iv. 16.) without being deterred by our crimes and abominations. Let us be convinced that Mary has been crowned Queen of mercy, it is that the greatest sinners may be saved by her intercession [b]." (p. 27, 28.) " Prayer in the mouth of a sinner— is useful and salutary, S. Thomas says, being founded not on the merits of him who prays, but on the goodness of God and the merits of Jesus Christ.—It is just the same with our petitions made in the name of His most holy Mother. If he who prays merits not to be heard, the merits of Mary will pray for him, says S. Anselm, exhorting all sinners to address themselves

[b] The shocking vision of the " two ladders," (see above, in Abp. Ussher, p. 203.) is repeated, p. 180.

confidently to—the Mother of God." (p. 51.) " S. Bernardine of Sienna asserts, that ' if God has not destroyed man after his sin, it was in consideration of—the blessed Virgin! and out of the singular love He bore her; he even doubts not that all the mercies granted to sinners in the old law have been given in consideration of—Mary! With good reason then does S. Bernard exhort us to seek grace through her since she has found the grace which we have lost. It is [not for herself, ' who needed it not, being by her' (immaculate) ' conception full of grace;' "] ' it is for sinners,' says Cardinal Hugo, ' that Mary has found grace, which they had irretrievably lost. Hence let them come, and say to her with confidence, render us what belongs to us." (p. 59.) " I shall no longer apprehend either my sins, since you can repair them; or the devils, since you are more powerful than hell; or your Son justly irritated, since one word from you will appease Him. I shall only fear myself, and that forgetting to invoke you, I shall be lost." (p. 74.) " If my Saviour drive me off because of my sins, I shall go and cast myself at the feet of His Mother; thence I shall not rise, until she has obtained my pardon; for she does not know what it is to be insensible to the voice of misery, and her pity will soften the anger of her Son. Regard us then, O Mary most merciful, for we your servants place all our hope in you." (p. 89.) " ' The sun,' says Hugo, ' is a figure of Jesus Christ, whose splendid rays illumine the just who live in the day of grace; the moon is typical of Mary, whose mild lustre illumines sinners amid the dreary night of sin.' ' It is towards this propitious orb,' says Innocent III., ' that he who is buried in the shades of iniquity should look.' Having lost divine grace, the day disappears, there is *no more sun for him;* but the moon is still on the horizon; let him address himself to Mary." (p. 91.) " ' This strong hold,' says Albertus M., ' is the sacred Virgin established in grace and glory.' Once introduced to her let us be silent, for it does not become us to open our mouth before the Lord, Whom we have so much offended, but leave Mary to speak and intercede for us." (p. 92.) " The glorious S. Bonaventure, to animate our confidence in Mary, represents to us a raging sea, in which sinners, already fallen from the vessel of divine grace, are tossed about by the billows of temptation, torn by the gnawings of remorse, and horrified by the terrors of Divine Justice. without light or guide, are ready to be swallowed up in the gulf of despair; but just then the Lord shews them Mary the star of the sea, and seems to say to them, ' Sinners, unfortunate sinners. despair not, fix your eyes on this bright luminary; its lustre will save you from the tempest, and conduct you to the port of salvation.' Blosius figures Mary to us, as the *only* refuge of those who have incurred the Divine indignation." (p. 93.) " The prophet complained—' Lord, we have sinned, and there is none to restrain your arm from falling heavy upon us;' but now Mary presents herself between God and His offending creatures.—Richard of S. Laurence also observes on this subject, that in the old law, God often complained that there was none to interpose between Him and sinners, but since Mary, the mediatrix of peace, has appeared on earth, she restrains His arm and averts His wrath." (p. 94.)　" S Anselm, in order to increase our confidence in Mary, assures us that our prayers will often be more speedily heard in invoking her name than in calling on that of Jesus Christ, and the reason he gives is, that Jesus being no less our Judge than our Saviour, He must avenge the wrongs we do Him by our sins, while the holy Virgin being solely our advocate, is obliged to entertain only sentiments of pity for us."

This is thus reconciled with the belief, which of course, Romanists must hold, that there is but " One Mediator between God and man."

" We are far from insinuating, *nevertheless*, that she is *more* powerful than her Son. Jesus Christ is our only Mediator; He alone has obtained our reconciliation with God His Father; but as in recurring to Him, Whom we must necessarily consider a Judge Who will punish the ungrateful, it is probable a sentiment of fear may lessen the confidence necessary for being heard, it would seem that in applying to Mary, whose office is that of mercy, our hope would be so strong as to obtain all we ask for." (p. 103.)

The explanation, however, leaves the fact as it was, that St. Mary is set forth as a more desirable Advocate than our Lord.

" How is it, that whereas we ask many things of God without obtaining them, we no sooner ask through Mary than they are granted us?" ib.

" As we have not access to The Father but by Jesus Christ, we have not access to Jesus Christ but through Mary, that this Divine Saviour Whom she has given to the world, may receive us from her hands. Who could know God except by you, O holy Virgin? who could be saved, O powerful Virgin, except through your intercession?" (p. 131.) Hugh of S. Victor exhorts us, if we are deterred by apprehension of the Divine Majesty, to approach to Mary without fear. She is, it is true, holy and spotless, the Queen of the Universe and the Mother of God, but she is also a pure creature, and a child of Adam like unto us. " If you fear to approach to God, look to Mary; then thou findest nothing to fear; thou seest thy own race." (p. 191.)

And these recommendations are enforced by the history of great sinners who were saved, having sought mercy of Mary alone.

" In my last moments, abandoned by all, and seeing myself loaded with sins, I addressed this prayer to the Mother of God, ' O thou, the refuge of the forsaken, have pity on me! Hope of the universe, my only hope, come to my assistance.' This little supplication was not made in vain. Mary obtained for me the grace of true contrition, by means of which I escaped Hell." (p. 40. see also p. 54—57.) "' I promised my Mother most readily (to recite the Rosary of the Blessed Virgin every day), and never failed to keep my word amid all my debaucheries; nay, I confess that for the last ten years it is the only act of religion I ever performed,' the confessor now saw clearly, that the conversion of this young man was owing to the special protection of Mary," (p. 90.)

These intercessions of S. Mary are represented also,

" As not only useful but necessary to this great end (our salvation), not of an absolute necessity, it is true, but of a moral necessity, which has its source in the Divine will." (p. 116.)

" Poor souls, what are you thinking of when you abandon Mary, when you cease crying to her for protection ? ' Take away the sun,' says S. Bernard, ' and what does the world become ? An abode of horror, a chaos of confusion; thus, let a soul abandon Mary, and she is seated in darkness, that darkness which the Holy Spirit says, ' favours the passage of the beasts of the forest.' ' Woe to him,' says S. Anselm, ' who despises the light of this sun, that is, who neglects Mary ; it is soon night with him, and his soul becomes a haunt of sin and of devils.' S. Francis Borgia doubted, and with reason, of the perseverance of such as had not a special devotion to Mary. Enquiring one day of the novices, to which saint each one was most devoted, he perceived, that some among them were wanting in devotion to the blessed Virgin, whereupon he noticed the master of novices, and desired him to have a particular watch on these young people. The event justified the saint's fears ; all those who had not honoured Mary, lost the grace of their vocation and quitted the society. S. Germanus then had reason to call Mary, ' the respiration of Christians ;' for as the body cannot exist without breathing, so the soul cannot live without recurring to the Mother of God.". (p. 67.)

" ' Blessed Virgin,' says S. Anselm, ' as it is impossible, that he who neglects and despises you, can be saved, so it is impossible, that he who has recourse to you sincerely, can be lost.' S. Antonius says, 'As those from whom Mary turns her merciful eyes, cannot be saved, it necessarily follows, that those on whom she looks with benignity, will share in eternal glory:' And here let us ask, if the words, ' It is impossible that he who is devout to Mary,' should not make those tremble, who despise or neglect her ? Let all such hear the anathema pronounced against them by Albertus Magnus; ' The people who will not serve you shall perish.' And S. Bonaventure, ' He who neglects Mary, shall die in his sins—he who does not invoke her, shall have no share in the kingdom of God ;' and again, ' There is no hope of salvation for those from whom Mary turns her face.'—" On the contrary, Mary assures us, that ' He who hears her, shall not be confounded.' S. Bonaventure says, ' Great Queen! he who perseveres in your service, is far from damnation.' ' No,' adds S. Hilary, ' he will not be lost, although he might have hitherto grievously offended his God." p. 167.

And thus not only is S. Mary held out to returning sinners as a Mediatrix more suited to them than our Lord, but as *the* special means, whereby they who stand may be kept upright.

" We have the same hope as this great saint, and shall not cease to say with S. Bonaventure, ' O Mary, I have hoped in you, and shall never be confounded." (p. 172.) S. Philip Neri used to say, ' My children, if you wish to persevere, be devout to Mary.' The venerable Berchman, S. J. said also, ' That he who loves Mary, will persevere to the end.' And Abbot Rupert draws from the parable of the prodigal a very ingenious reflection to the same effect. ' If this libertine child,' said he, ' had his Mother, he would never have abandoned his paternal home, or he would have returned sooner:' thus he who has Mary for Mother, never abandons God, or if he does, he soon seeks Him again. Oh if all men loved this most merciful Mother, and had recourse to her in the hour of temptation, we would seldom see any one lost, or suffer shipwreck.' We fall, and we are lost, when we fail to invoke her assistance. Saint Laurence Justinian applies to the blessed Virgin these words of Ecclesiasticus, ' I walked on the waves of the sea ;' for he makes her say, ' I walk on the waves of the sea with my servants, in order to save them from a melancholy shipwreck.' S. Thomas Villanova says, ' When the birds of prey (meaning the devils) pounce on us, let us imitate the chickens, who when the hawk appears, fly for refuge under the wings of their Mother ; let us fly to Mary without losing a moment, and she will secure us in her maternal bosom. O Mary, continues the saint, addressing the Queen of heaven; it is for you to defend us, since you after God are our refuge, our protectress, our sweetest hope.' We shall conclude with the words of S. Bernard: ' Christian whoever thou art, thy life on earth is a perilous navigation : if thou dost not wish to be drowned, turn not away thy eyes from this brilliant star, look up at the star of mariners, invoke Mary in occasions of sin, in the struggle of temptation, in the midst of danger call Mary to thy aid; let her powerful name be ever in thy heart, and on thy lips, to inspire thee with confidence; trust in Mary, and thou wilt not fall into despair; follow her, and thou wilt not stray; let her hand protect thee, and thou wilt have nothing to fear; let her be thy guide, and thou wilt infallibly arrive at the haven of salvation. This do, and thou shalt live." (p. 69—71.) " The Church in her public service teaches us to recur to Mary under the titles of Health of the sick; Refuge of sinners; Help of Christians. In her offices for the festivals of Mary, she applies to her these words of Wisdom : ' In me is all hope of life and virtue ;' again, ' he who finds me shall find life, and obtain salvation from the Lord : they who work in me shall have life everlasting.' Now what do all those texts go to prove, but that the intercession of Mary is necessary for us ?"

Lastly, it should be noticed that there is an essential difference between the way in which men's salvation is in any passages of the fathers said to be derived through S. Mary, and that in which it is attributed to her by these later writers. The object of S. Irenæus[c] and other fathers, in the first place, is not to magnify S. Mary, but to point out the reality of the Incarnation, which was denied by the Gnostic heretics; but then, further, the benefits are said to be derived through her, in that, of her according to the flesh, Christ was born; in the later writers, they are attributed to her by virtue of the dignity, *since* bestowed upon her: in the fathers, they are spoken as coming from her indirectly, in later writers, directly; in the fathers, from her when on earth, in later writers from her in Heaven; in the fathers from the Nativity of our Lord, later, from *her* sovereignty, rule, Intercession, Command,

[c] " This comparison between Mary and Eve (' that the world is freed by [through] a Virgin, which before by a virgin [Eve] had fallen under sin,') in the same manner as Christ and Adam are compared, is so common among the older writers, that from S. Irenæus downwards, it would be easy to fill pages with quotations." Dr. Wiseman's remarks on Mr. Palmer's Letter, p. 24.

with which for her merits she is alleged to be invested. The expressions of the fathers do not go beyond St. Paul's words, " Adam was not deceived, but, the woman being deceived was in the transgression ; notwithstanding, she shall be saved through the childbearing," as though the blessed fact that our Lord was " born of a woman" had some mysterious relation to the fall by a woman ; that there is a correspondence between death coming through the transgression of the woman and life coming through her.   In the " Glories of Mary" it is expressly denied that this is the sense in which the modern sayings should be taken.

" That God has constituted Mary the ordinary dispensatrix of His graces, was the opinion of St. Bernard : it is now the common opinion of all theologians, and all doctors.   It is taught by Tega, Mendozza, Poire, Pacciucbelli, Segneri, Crásset, and a crowd of others.   Even Father Noel Alexander, so reserved in his propositions, says, ' That God wishes that all the favours men expect from Him, they should be indebted for to the intercession of Mary.' "
" But this doctrine does not please a certain modern author : this person, who otherwise speaks with much piety and learning, of true and false devotion, is very parsimonious when there is question of the worship of the holy Virgin, refusing her that glory, and those privileges, which a St. Germanus, a St. Anselm, a St. John Damascene, St. Bonaventure, a St. Antonius, a St. Bernardine of Sienna, and innumerable othe, holy doctors, made no difficulty to grant her.   He pretends that the aforesaid proposition, ' God confers no grace but through Mary's intercession,' is an hyperbole which fervour caused some saints to utter, and that it is only correct in this sense, that ' Mary has given to the world, Jesus the Author of grace;' for, adds ne, ' the apostle formally teaches, that we acknowledge but One sole Mediator between God and man, viz. the Word made flesh." (p. 116, 7.)

It is for earnest-minded Romanists seriously to consider the tendency of all this ; Faith is not holding truth in the abstract, it must penetrate the life and run through a man's whole belief; worldly-minded persons are often, in the whole habit of their mind, Socinians, although if asked they would acknowledge or think that they believed the Divinity and Atonement of our Lord ; and persons may be practically worshippers of the Blessed Virgin only, while they would acknowledge in the abstract that she derives all her power from her Son.   It ought probably to awaken some fears in them that they habitually contemplate and speak of S. Mary as " the Mother of God" only, still speak of our Lord, in reference to her, as her Son only ; there may be in this a subtle Humanitarianism, which, while they are encouraged to shrink from the thought of their Lord as their Judge, thinks of Him only as the Son of Mary, and while it acknowledges S. Mary as the Mother of God, practically forgets that He created her, and in that they hold her to have been without sin, denies that He redeemed her.   The term " Mother of God" expresses Catholic truth ; yet may it be, and it is, continually used by Romanists in an heretical sense.

While these things are so, although we did not separate from Rome, yet since God has permitted that Rome should separate us from her, we see not how the Anglican Church could re-unite with her, without betraying the trust which she owes to her own children.

THE END.

BAXTER, PRINTER, OXFORD.